Hidden France

Richard Binns

D1331273

CORGI

Abbreviations

fpm   range of cost of fixed price menus

meals   evening meal compulsory – C: not compulsory – NC. Note, however, that recent government legislation requires establishments to offer bedroom without demanding that clients dine in their restaurants

rooms   number of bedrooms and price band range (all hotels have some bedroom with baths or showers unless otherwise stated)

closed   annual and weekly dates of closing (a **caveat**: always try to check ahead)

post   local post code, Village or Town, *département*

phone   area code (in brackets) and telephone number. **In 1986 area codes become an integral part of all French phone numbers**

Price Bands

A	50 to 100 Francs	C	150 to 200 Francs
B	100 to 150 Francs	D	200 to 250 Francs
	E	Over 250 Francs	

(All price bands include service charges and taxes: wine is not included in meal price bands, nor are breakfasts included in room price bands)

Maps

Villages and Towns in which recommended hotels are located are shown on the area maps as follows: ● SAMATAN

Within each of the 25 areas these villages and towns are listed alphabetically on the final page of the area chapter. Example:

Name of Village/Town   Name of Hotel
SAMATAN   Maigné

Villages and Towns in which *French Leave* recommended hotels and restaurants are located are shown as follows (over 150 appear on the 25 area maps): ● AUCH
Some offer really good value for money cuisine or have other attractive features (see *French Leave*) – these are shown on area maps as follows: ● PLAISANCE

Places of special interest – towns, villages, rivers and other scenic attractions – referred to in each area text (in **bold** print) are shown on each area map as follows
●**Pau**   ●**Madiran**   ●**Nogaro**   *Gers*   *Adour*   LANDES
Some are real favourites of mine and deserve special emphasis – **don't miss** them
These are shown in each area text and on each area map as follows: ● Fourcès

INTRODUCTION

Hidden France is for the independent, discerning traveller who recognises the rewarding benefits that accrue when one gets off the beaten track and well away from package-holiday traps. That enterprise allows one to savour the sights, sounds and tastes of rural France: its woods and forests; its meadows and pastures; its hills and river valleys; its placid streams and roaring torrents; its ancient villages and medieval buildings; and its vast larder of culinary delights.

Many of the most beautiful parts of France are amongst the least visited – for all practical purposes they remain *hidden* to the huge majority of visitors; areas of attractive countryside where one can breathe fresh air and where Mother Nature has fashioned many priceless treasures. Brother Roger of Taizé put it simply with these words: *the constant need to admire is satisfied.*

I have chosen 25 areas in France, each one of which demonstrates perfectly the pleasure and joy you can win for yourself when you seek out the hidden corners of that enchanting country. It is a subjective, idiosyncratic list; I would have loved to extend it, but within the limits of cost I set for myself, I had to settle for just 25. In each area I have tried to highlight for you what makes it attractive – detailing scenic, artistic and culinary pleasures.

Every one of the 25 areas is in unspoilt country – but to enjoy them to the full you must recognise three prerequisites. Firstly, acknowledge the huge dividends a car can bring when it is used intelligently and with enterprise. Secondly, realise that you must often desert your car to savour the myriad pleasures of Nature: it's your legs that will take you to the finest viewpoints, the banks of tranquil streams, across a bracing moor or through a still, cool wood. Expose all your senses this way – that's not always possible sitting in a car! Finally, accept without question that a good large-scale map will repay its small outlay a thousand times over. Immerse yourself in maps – pore over them; every hour spent studying them will be time wisely spent. I count myself fortunate that I have always had an enthusiastic passion for maps and navigation.

All place names in **bold** print in *Hidden France* are identified on the accompanying area maps; the names of all wines and cheeses are highlighted in **bold** print also – refer to the indexes in *French Leave*. Each area map indicates the number of the Michelin yellow map(s) that you should refer to for greater detail.

In each of the 25 areas four recommended hotels are described – inexpensive, modest, family-owned establishments. Not one of them will bankrupt you – there is always one to suit any budget. **Not one of the 100 has a Michelin star for cooking; don't expect too much in that area – what you will find is a reasonable standard of good-value cuisine.** The symbol **GC** indicates good cooking – where standards are higher than average. (If you want cuisine of the really highest level, use the *French Leave* recommendations which are clearly indicated on each of the 25 area maps: *Gers* is the perfect example; there are seven superb *French Leave* recommendations to supplement the four entries in this book.) Many of the 100 entries are *Logis de France* hotels and the majority have quiet sites. Be **sure** to read page 2.

Richard Binns resigned from a successful career in computers in 1980 to become a do-it-yourself publisher with his first book *French Leave*. The success of this title – it zoomed up the *Sunday Times'* Bestseller list – led to more successes in the guidebook field with *France à la Carte, Hidden France* and *Best of Britain*. He will publish *French Leave Favourites* in November 1986 and is currently working on a guide to French Autoroutes.

A self-acknowledged Francophile and 'Mapoholic' he marries his enthusiasm and zest for travel with an unflinching honesty when it comes to recommending hotels and restaurants. He now receives hundreds of letters every year about his books which help him in his research. When not exploring France he lives in Amersham, Bucks with his wife and two grown-up children.

NOTE FROM THE AUTHOR

As some of my readers may know, I originally published *Hidden France* as a do-it-yourself publishing venture. In a way the success of my publishing on my own has led to this Corgi edition of *Hidden France*, published together with *French Leave 3, France à la Carte* and *Best of Britain* for I found the pressures of being a publisher meant that I had too little time to devote to the research and writing of my books and, by doing all the distribution myself, I found I was not reaching a large enough market. A problem now partly solved to allow me to research and write my two forthcoming titles: *French Leave Favourites* (to be published by Chiltern House in a limited hardback edition) and *French Autoroutes* (to be exclusively published by Corgi Books).

A CORGI BOOK 0 552 99230 5

Originally published in Great Britain by Chiltern House Publishers Limited, Chiltern House, Amersham Road, Amersham, Bucks HP6 5PE

PRINTING HISTORY
Chiltern House edition published 1982
Corgi revised edition published 1986

Copyright © Richard Binns 1982, 1986 (Text, Photographs, Illustrations and Maps)

All the photographs reproduced in *Hidden France* were taken by the author during the period March to May 1982. The weather was not always kind, as a result the quality of some photographs suffered. Cover photograph the chateau at Sediere (see *Correze*) – taken by the author in March 1982.
Editing assistance Jane Watson
Maps by Richard Binns and H. Plews Gregory. Illustrations by Richard Binns.

This book is set in Century

Corgi Books are published by Transworld Publishers Ltd., Century House, 61–63 Uxbridge Road, Ealing, London W5 5SA, in Australia by Transworld Publishers (Aust.) Pty. Ltd., 26 Harley Crescent, Condell Park, NSW 2200, and in New Zealand by Transworld Publishers (N.Z.) Ltd., Cnr. Moselle and Waipareira Avenues, Henderson, Auckland.
Typeset by Art Photoset Limited, 64 London End, Beaconsfield, Bucks.

Printed in West Germany by Mohndruck, Gütersloh.

CONTENTS

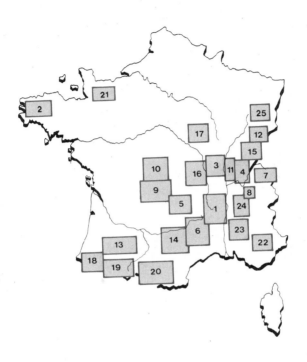

ARDECHE

1

Loire

Lignon

Annonay ●

Cance

ST-VALLIER ●

SATILLIEU ●

Lalouvesc ●

Doux

TAIN-L'HERMITAGE ●

TOURNON ●

● **TENCE**

Montagne du Meygal ▲

LE CHAMBON-SUR-LIGNON

● Gorges de Peyredeyre

Le Puy ●

St-Agrève ●

LAMASTRE ●

PONT-DE-L'ISERE ◄

ST-ROMAIN-DE-LERPS ●

ST-PERAY ●

VALENCE ●

Solignac-s-Loire ●

Le Monastier ●

● Goudet

▲ Mont Mézenc

La Voulte-s-Rhône ●

Arlempdes ●

Lac-d'Issarlès ●

▲ Gerbier de Jonc

Ray-Pic ● ●

● Burzet

THUEYTS

VALS-LES-BAINS ●

Cruas ●

Masméjean ●

Col de la Croix de Bauzon ●

● Aubenas

Chenavari ▲

Borne ●

Col de Meyrand ●

Lignon

Rochemaure

St-Laurent-les-Bains ●

● **VALGORGE**

Montélimar ●

Borne

● Thines

Chassezac

Joyeuse ●

Ardèche

Les Vans ● ●

Bois de Paiolive

● Vallon-Pont-d'Arc

Gorges de l'Ardèche

Rhône

Aven d'Orgnac ●

Barjac ●

Pont-St-Esprit ●

*Michelin maps 76 & 80
see page 37*

Why is it that this delightful area of France – most of it contained within the boundaries of the Ardèche *département* – is probably known to one in 10,000 of the motorists speeding down the A7? For me it represents the classic example of what treasures can be discovered in *Hidden France*; what makes this area so special is that most of the great sights you'll see have been fashioned by Mother Nature – in a multitude of different ways.

The Ardèche repays a handsome dividend whether you invest several days of your time or, alternatively, if you just spend one day there, as you travel south to holiday destinations, or when you return north, homeward bound. I find I am always eager to seek out some new hidden corner; you, too, will be enchanted and will return often to these secret, tree-covered hills.

Annonay is the perfect gateway to the Ardèche; but, so that you can discover exactly what I mean when I implore you to study maps beforehand, don't approach the town from the north-east, via the N82. Instead, search out the minute D270 that hugs the banks of the River **Cance** from the point it joins the mighty **Rhône**, just north of **St-Vallier**. The D270 approaches Annonay from the south-east and what an enjoyable *entrée* it will be for you to the Ardèche.

Leave Annonay to the south via the D578A. From **Satillieu** the road climbs steeply up into the hills to **Lalouvesc** – beyond, use the narrow lanes that take you south-west, principally the D214 towards **St-Agrève** and then to **La Chambon-s-Lignon**. At any time of the year this is memorable country: I've seen it in midwinter when rallying was the sole reason for being there – snow and ice, and tight schedules, allowed me no time to stand and stare; in spring my wife and I have thrilled at the new greens bursting into life and the first wild flowers opening in the high meadows; but the season of the year I remember most vividly is early autumn. Even today, years later, I can recall in particular a warm, cloudless Sunday, when every lane, every pasture, every wood and hill was bathed in clear, flawless autumn light – the sort of day when you wished time would stand still.

The **Lignon** Valley between Le Chambon-s-Lignon and **Tence** is a special delight. Explore both sides of this attractive stretch of wooded river country; then strike west with the objective of using the roads to the immediate north of the **Montagne du Meygal** – you'll enjoy a succession of fine views, to north, south and west. Eventually descend towards **Le Puy**.

Before driving into this dramatically-sited town, detour north, using the D103 that hugs the **Loire** as it flows downstream through the **Gorges de Peyredeyre**. You will see more of the young Loire later as you follow it upstream towards its source – but the reason for this short detour is for you to thrill at the sight of the Château Lavoûte-Polignac; it has a remarkable and romantic site, sitting on a volcanic rock which falls vertically to the river below. This landscape was described by George Sand in 1859 as a *site grandoise*.

Le Puy is one of the most unusual towns in France. Sharp needles of volcanic rock rise on all sides, several of them having chapels and statues on their summits. The most needle-like has the Chapelle St-Michel d'Aiguilhe on its peak – a Romanesque chapel worthy of the 267 step climb to reach it. Another outcrop has the huge statue of Notre Dame de France on its summit. The cathedral is a strange mixture of Byzantine and Romanesque; the cloisters are particularly cool, quiet and

8   The Ardèche south of Vallon-Pont-d'Arc: a natural arch formed by the river

inspiring and are amongst the finest in France.

The Rhône Valley country, far to the east, will already have given you the chance to try some of its fine wines; here in the Velay hills you'll not enjoy any *local* wines – but look out for the yellow and green liqueurs called **Verveine du Velay**; they include over 30 plants, such as wild verbena, that grow in the mountains encircling Le Puy. Green Puy lentils are served with sausages – an ideal accompaniment would be the red wines from the **Côtes d'Auvergne**, to the north-west of Le Puy. *French Leave* lists many of the regional specialities of the Massif Central and provides details of all its wines and cheeses.

It is not possible to follow the banks of the infant River Loire all the way to its source; but there are many places where you'll catch sight of the torrent. First from **Solignac-s-Loire**; then cross the river and climb to **Le Monastier**, where Robert Louis Stevenson started his travels, in 1878, with Modestine (he bought the old animal there), later made famous in his book *Travels with a Donkey in the Cévennes*. Recross the Loire at **Goudet** and circle round to **Arlempdes**, on the west bank – it has a dramatic site, château ruins and a tremendous view. Continue via the **Lac-d'Issarlès** – its waters are an intense blue – to a point where the first trickle of the newly-born Loire emerges, under the shadow of the round-topped summit of a mountain called the **Gerbier de Jonc**.

Use the roads that encircle both the Gerbier de Jonc and **Mont Mézenc** – extensive views lie in all directions. Make a detour to the south to the **Ray-Pic** cascade – the short walk from the roadside parking area rewards you with a close-up view of its foaming fall. In late spring there is no more enchanting diversion – the pastures to the south of the Gerbier de Jonc are a mass of colour; the woods are a delight – a mixture of evergreens and deciduous trees. The river scenes near **Burzet** are a thrilling spectacle, particularly after heavy rains.

Close examination of the right hand corner of Michelin map 76 will show you clearly why it is such splendid rally country – the narrow, exacting roads are perfect for competition motoring. You'll be taking it easy, stopping frequently to enjoy a view; use as many of the lanes that you can but generally head north-east towards **Lamastre**. Between Lamastre and **Valence** is one of the most exciting and extensive viewpoints in the Ardèche, at **St-Romain-de-Lerps**.

Desert your car at nearby **Tournon** and revel in the pleasure that will be yours when you use the best of all the privately-owned steam railways in France. The Chemin de Fer du Vivarais runs from Tournon to Lamastre; it's a metre gauge line that follows the **Doux** Valley on its 33 kilometre journey – it climbs 250 metres in the process. It runs every day in June, July and August; Saturday and Sunday in September and Sunday only in October.

After enjoying that, head south from **St-Péray**. On the craggy rocks to the east of the town are the ruins of the Château de Crussol; further south, high above **La Voulte-s-Rhône** are more ruins – those of the Château de Pierre-Gourde. The climb rewards you with a spectacular view. If you continue due south, following the west bank of the Rhône, other sites will entice you: first **Cruas**, with its *église* and recently discovered crypts; the views from the **Chenavari** peak; and, below it, the ruins of the medieval village and château at **Rochemaure**. Don't be put off by the hideous power station near these sites.

Now head west again – to the seclusion and peace of the high hills. You'll notice how the lush greens of the north have changed to the drier, more scrub-like vegetation of the south. Your first objective is **Aubenas**; and then **Vals-les-Bains**, a pleasant enough small spa town; but it is the route that follows that I am anxious you use. It's a spectacular run with thrills a plenty and you'll pass through villages where time appears to have stood still.

From Vals-les-Bains follow the River **Ardèche** to the west; then climb the **Lignon** Valley to the **Col de la Croix de Bauzon**. Three kilometres beyond its summit make the *deviation* through **Masméjean** and along the *dead-end* D301 to **Borne** in the **Borne** Valley. Return to the **Col de Meyrand** with its splendid views. Five kilometres later bear right on the D403, at the point you change to Michelin map number 80. At **St-Laurent-les-Bains** re-enter the Borne Valley and follow the tiny lanes that go due south along its river banks until it joins the River **Chassezac**. Continue along the latter's northern bank, but be certain to detour to **Thines**; an attractive church and a pretty drive will be your reward. Pass through **Les Vans**, then use the D901 and the tiny D252 that heads east through the **Bois de Païolive** – unusual rock formations and weird trees line the road.

Two final and essential objectives remain. Near **Barjac**, to the south-east of Les Vans, is the **Aven d'Orgnac**, an astonishing cave with colossal stalagmites and mighty halls. Visit that thrilling sight, then head north to **Vallon-Pont-d'Arc** and, following the D290 **Gorges de l'Ardèche** road that runs south-east, high above the River Ardèche, enjoy the breathtaking 47 kilometre drive to **Pont-St-Esprit**, one of the finest in France.

LE CHAMBON-SUR-LIGNON   Clair Matin
Simple hotel/Secluded/Gardens/Swimming pool/Tennis

The countryside surrounding Le Chambon-sur-Lignon is a plateau – full of woods and streams. This modern chalet-style *Logis de France* has a tranquil site, nestling amongst pine trees; it is well to the east of the small town and its slightly elevated position provides extensive views to the west. It's an ideal spot to enjoy walking, riding and fishing in this verdant hill country.
fpm A *meals* NC *rooms* 28 A–D *closed* 1–15 Oct. Mid Nov–mid Mar.
post 43400 Le Chambon-sur-Lignon. H.-Loire. *phone* (71) 59.73.03.

SATILLIEU   Gentilhommière
Comfortable hotel/Quiet/Gardens/Swimming pool/Tennis

What an attractive site; the hotel is south-west of the village on the **Lalouvesc** road – it's surrounded by trees and has every facility you could need. Dense pine forests cover the high hills to the west and south; the many chestnut trees to the north-east provide a flourishing local trade – witness the delicious *marrons glacés* and, in another form, *the purée de marrons*.
fpm A–D *meals* NC *rooms* 11 D–E *closed* Rest only: 1 Nov–mid Mar.
post 07290 Satillieu. Ardèche. *phone* (75) 34.94.31.

THUEYTS   Nord
Comfortable hotel/Gardens

The River **Ardèche** starts its life a few kilometres to the west of this small village. There's a fine view of the river from a point just east of the hotel. You'll find marvellous river country to the north: don't miss **Burzet** and the Cascade du **Ray-Pic**; and the infant stream called the **Loire**. Enjoy *truite au Champagne* and *tarte aux myrtilles* – two of the restaurant's specialities.
fpm A–B *meals* C *rooms* 25 B–D *closed* Mid Oct–Easter. Mon (out of season).
post 07330 Thueyts. Ardèche. *phone* (75) 36.40.38.

VALGORGE   Le Tanargue
Comfortable hotel/Secluded/Gardens/Lift

This modern *Logis* is away from the main village street. Follow the narrow lanes alongside the River Beaume to **Joyeuse** – enjoy the splendid forests that lie to the north of **Les Vans**. Seek out the jewel of **Thines** (another *dead-end* road) and the extensive views from the **Col de Meyrand**. Dishes here include local *jambon cru* and *saucisson, truites* and *caille Cévenole*.
fpm A–B *meals* NC *rooms* 25 C–D *closed* Jan. Feb.
post Valgorge, 07110 Largentière. Ardèche. *phone* (75) 35.68.88.

11

2

La Roche ●

● St-Thégonnec
● Lampaul-Guimiliau

La Martyre ●

Guimiliau

Plougastel-Daoulas ●

● Sizun

PARC REGIONAL D'AMORIQUE

▲ Roc Trévezel

MONTS D'ARREE ▲   HUELGOAT ●

Landévennec ● ● LE FAOU   Montagne St-Michel   LOCMARIA

Ménez-Hom

PORT LAUNAY

Plomodiern ●

● Pleyben

CHATEAULIN   CHATEAUNEUF-DU-FAOU

STE-ANNE-LA-PALUD   Spézet

Trévarez ●   Roc de Toullaër

● Locronan   Forêt de Laz

MONTAGNES NOIRES

● QUIMPER

● ROSPORDEN

Many of you will not immediately identify – from the title alone – just where this strangely-named area is situated; the map of course will give you the clues you need, but even they are not too obvious. Lovers of Brittany will know that *Argoat* – in Breton – means *wooded country* or the *land of the woods*; the superb coast of Brittany is called the *Armor* – the *land of the sea*. Thus, the map alongside will now make sense to you: inland Brittany is where I will try to tempt you to spend some time on your next holiday in the region; sadly it is an area neglected by most holidaymakers.

Inland Brittany is hardly *wooded* any longer; centuries ago there were huge expanses of oak and beech covering the hills and plateaux. Small pockets of delightful forest do still exist, but, for the most part, it is a countryside dominated by heathland and moors in the central areas. To the north, east and south you'll find great tracts of farmland – a vast chess-board of fields. Windy the whole area may well be – witness the smallish fields, surrounded by hedges, earthen dykes or trees (known as *bocage*) – but it is also warmed by the Gulf Stream and this priceless legacy of Nature has made it into one of the market-gardens of France. Artichokes, cauliflowers, peas, beans, onions, potatoes and magnificent strawberries from **Plougastel** (the top left-hand corner of my map) are amongst the crops harvested in this rich greenhouse.

You'll notice that my map shows little of the Breton coastline. Yet, to north, south and west, it's only a few kilometres away; you have the advantage that any part of this thrilling coast can easily be reached – and a bonus is that all the treasures harvested daily from the sea are also available for you to savour inland. Sole, turbot,

Michelin map 230

bass, mackerel, lobster, oysters, scallops, clams, mussels – these are just some of the immense variety of fish and shellfish available to the housewife and chef alike. You'll enjoy them cooked in many ways; perhaps in a *cotriade* – the Breton fish stew made from a number of whatever fish are available, combined with potatoes, onions, sometimes garlic, butter and cream.

You will have many opportunities to relish other regional specialities: *galettes* – where buckwheat flour is used to make tasty pancakes that come with a variety of savoury fillings; *crêpes* – made from wheat flour with sweet fillings and often called *crêpes au froment*; *far Breton* – a batter mixture with a raisin filling; *gâteau Breton* – a mouthwatering concoction of butter, egg yolks, sugar and flour. If all that is not enough there are some marvellous pork products – particularly good are the hams from Morlaix, off the northern edge of my map; and finally *poulet blanc Breton* – free-range white Breton chicken.

I make no apologies for highlighting many of the gastronomic pleasures of the area first – throughout France that aspect of discovery is certainly no less pleasing than the more normal visual sights. Certainly the Argoat is not endowed with a heritage of man-made architectural treasures – rather it is graced with a series of kindlier, less spectacular pleasures where Mother Nature has fashioned the textures and colours that will fill your eyes. I love it best in late spring; the air is clear and sharp, the new greens of spring are emerging at every turn, golden splashes of broom and gorse blanket the moors, and every building seems to be a freshly whitewashed one.

Start by exploring a ring of country surrounding **Huelgoat** You won't find it by accident – you must make a deliberate effort to seek it out. It's bang in the middle of the **Parc Régional d'Armorique**, one of France's glorious Regional Nature Parks. To the north are hills called **Monts d'Arrée** and to the south the **Montagnes Noires**; but don't be deceived, as they are not mountains to be compared with the magnificent specimens on the south-east border of France. At their highest points they are just under 400 metres above sea-level. The best parts of the Monts d'Arrée encircle Huelgoat: the hills here are carpeted with forests of oak, spruce, pine and beech; scattered within them are huge blocks of granite and sandstone – there are many rock formations worth exploring. Clearly it is a paradise for walkers; your car and your independence have brought you to this exquisite hidden corner, but to reap the best of it, you must use your feet and lungs – you will not regret a second of it. Equally, it is also a paradise for fishermen with many streams and a lake as an added bonus; ask locally about permits.

What do those two mountain areas hide within their wind-swept, deserted heights? Vast panoramic views will be yours if you search out the **Montagne St-Michel** and particularly the **Roc Trévezel** – both are to the west of Huelgoat and both summits are very easy indeed to reach on foot.

From those craggy summits you will see distant views of the countryside surrounding several villages – villages which you must certainly now seek out. It's in these villages that you will discover examples of the unique *enclos paroissiaux* (parish enclosures); calvaries, where scores of centuries-old sculptures fill the cemeteries and churchyards. You will not see anything like it elsewhere in France; some of the best examples lie to the north of the Roc Trévezel – at **St-Thégonnec**,

14   The lake at Huelgoat

Lampaul-Guimiliau, Guimiliau and **Plougonven**. Another marvellous one is at **Plougastel-Daoulas** – strawberry country – on the western edge of the map. Others in this north-west corner are at **La Roche, La Martyre** and **Sizun**. To the south of the Monts d'Arrée is **Pleyben**, where there is another splendid 400 year old calvary – one of the largest and best examples in Brittany. The churches in all these villages are also well worth exploring.

The Montagnes Noires are lower than the Arrée hills to the north and they show a different and deserted face of the Breton countryside. The highest point is the **Roc de Toullaëron**, 326 metres high; again the summit can be reached on foot. The best part of this hilly ridge of country is in the west – just south of **Châteauneuf-du-Faou**. Seek out the **Forêt de Laz** and there is a delightful forest park at **Trévarez**, at its best in spring when the rhododendrons and azaleas are at their best. You'll get fine views of the **Aulne** Valley to the north of the hills, from the nearby Point de vue de Laz. There's a church with splendid stained glass windows near **Spézet** – it's called the Notre Dame du Crann.

The River Aulne bisects the two ranges of hills. I am particularly fond of it; in its short life from the point where it rises, north-east of Huelgoat, to its estuary in the west, it's a river of many parts. Much of its early life is spent gurgling amongst the woods I described earlier; in its middle age, east and west of Châteauneuf-du-Faou (a pretty place, overlooking the river) it's a lazier version. It's renowned for its salmon. The stretch of river from Châteauneuf-du-Faou downstream to **Châteaulin** is full of salmon from April to July. Châteaulin's main attraction is indeed its riverside quays; the river to the north is at its best for salmon fishing during the first three months of the year. The sight of the leaping salmon, fighting to climb upstream, is particularly good in the stretches between the two towns and, needless to say, this is yet another speciality of the restaurants hereabouts during the first half of the year.

Be certain to make the drive up to the top of **Ménez-Hom**. From the 330 metres high viewpoint your eyes will be filled with the varying scenic aspects that make Brittany so rewarding: the sea to the west; the gentle hills to the east; and the placid, lovely Aulne Estuary to the north. Explore the lanes that line its banks and later the villages of **Landévennec** and ancient **Le Faou**. To the south of Menez-Hom is **Locronan** with its dark granite houses, its church and more extensive views from the hills above the town.

What else remains of this exquisite inland part of Brittany? Well, for my money the **Lac de Guerlédan** is one of the best of all the attractions; it's a glorious expanse of water and immediately to the south is another fine forest, the **Forêt de Quénécan**. There are many splendid natural sights, pretty viewpoints and charming old villages in the neighbourhood to please you. There are three gorges to seek out: at the western end of the lake are the **Gorges du Daoulas**; further upstream on the **Blavet** are the **Gorges de Toul Goulic**; and just west of the latter are the **Gorges du Corong**. All are easy to reach – the last named will require a good walk on your part. Explore **Carhaix-Plouguer**. Then continue in a loop to a handful of small villages to the north-east; they will reward you richly if you want countryside to yourself – **Plourac'h, Callac, Bulat-Pestivien** and **Locarn**; all have small ancient chapels and churches.

16   Le Faou: a handsome restored old house

CHATEAULIN   Aub. Ducs de Lin
Comfortable restaurant with rooms/Quiet/Gardens/GC

A small place high above the **Aulne** to the south of the town. Inevitably salmon appears on the menu as do *huîtres, homard, gratin de crabe* and *filet de sole*. As an alternative for rooms use the Ferme de Porz-Morvan just a few kilometres to the west at **Plomodiern** (postcode 29127). *Sans restaurant*, it is a truly delightful, secluded spot – a restored farmhouse. It also has a tennis court.

fpm A–E *meals* C *rooms* 6 D *closed* 1–15 Mar. Mid Sept–mid Oct. Mon (but not hotel in July–Aug). *post* 29150 Châteaulin. Finistère. *phone* (98) 86.04.20.

CHATEAUNEUF-DU-FAOU   Relais de Cornouaille
Very simple hotel (no showers or baths)

On the eastern side of the town; extensive views from the rear that include the church called Notre Dame des Portes and the **Montagnes Noires** on the far, southern side of the **Aulne**. Fish dishes dominate the menu: *huîtres, palourdes, crevettes, raie au beurre noisette, saumon beurre blanc, lotte* and *limande sole Grenobloise*. Simple it may all be but you can't get better value than this.

fpm A *meals* C *rooms* 8 A *closed* Oct. Sat. Sun evg.
post 29119 Châteauneuf-du-Faou. Finistère. *phone* (98) 81.75.36.

LE FAOU   Vieille Renommée
Comfortable hotel/Lift

Both this modern hotel and its neighbour the Relais de la Place offer really fine value for money; competition of that sort keeps them both on their toes. (This is also true of the two main hotels in **Rosporden**, to the south.) Apart from the obvious delights like *moules marinière, sole meunière* and *langoustines mayonnaise*, there are other non-fish dishes: *pintadeau rôti, andouillette* and *faux-filet*.

fpm A–C *meals* NC *rooms* 38 B–D *closed* 1–15 Sept. Mid–end Oct. Feb. Mon (except July–Aug). *post* 29142 Le Faou. Finistère. *phone* (98) 81.90.31.

PORT LAUNAY   Au Bon Accueil
Comfortable hotel/Lift

A whitewashed, modern place overlooking the **Aulne**, downstream from **Châteaulin**. Madame Le Guillou, the owner, has won her considerable reputation after years of careful development. Salmon from the Aulne features on the menu, as do *moules, sole, langouste* and *homard*. *Sole braisée au Vermouth* is a well-known speciality of the hotel. But what about *Le Mutton 'Shop' à la sauge* – sounds great!

fpm A–E *meals* C *rooms* 59 A–D *closed* Jan. Rest only: Mon (mid Sept–Apl).
post Port Launay. 29150 Châteaulin. Finistère. *phone* (98) 86.15.77.

BEAUJOLAIS

3

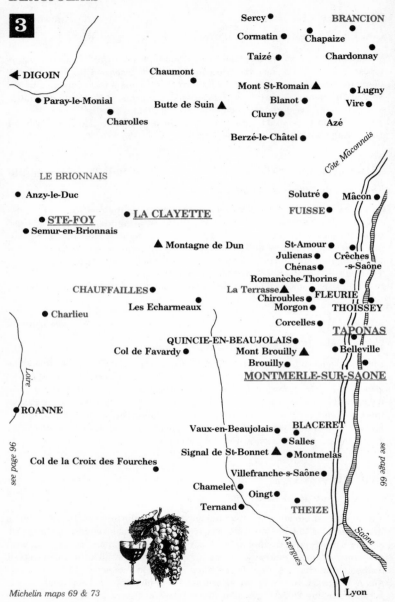

Sercy ●

BRANCION

Cormatin ● Chapaize ●

Taizé ● Chardonnay ●

◀ DIGOIN

Chaumont ●

Mont St-Romain ▲ ● Lugny

● Paray-le-Monial

Butte de Suin ▲ Blanot ● Vire ●

Charolles ● Cluny ● Azé ●

Berzé-le-Châtel ●

Côte Mâconnais

LE BRIONNAIS

● Anzy-le-Duc

Solutré ● Mâcon ●

● STE-FOY ● LA CLAYETTE

FUISSE ●

● Semur-en-Brionnais

▲ Montagne de Dun

St-Amour ●

Julienas ● Crêches

Chénas ● -s-Saône

CHAUFFAILLES ●

Romanèche-Thorins ●

La Terrasse ▲ FLEURIE

● Charlieu

Les Echarmeaux ●

Chiroubles ● THOISSEY

Morgon ●

Corcelles ● TAPONAS

QUINCIE-EN-BEAUJOLAIS ●

Col de Favardy ● Mont Brouilly ▲ ● Belleville

Brouilly ●

MONTMERLE-SUR-SAONE

Loire

● ROANNE

BLACERET

Vaux-en-Beaujolais ●

● Salles

Signal de St-Bonnet ▲ ● Montmelas

Col de la Croix des Fourches ●

Villefranche-s-Saône ●

Chamelet ● Oingt ●

THEIZE

Ternand ●

Saône

Azergues

Lyon

Michelin maps 69 & 73

18

see page 96

see page 96

Most tourists would not consider putting aside some days to explore this corner of France. The name **Beaujolais** would, in most minds, be associated with a pleasant enough red wine – but they would know little else about the topography that the map encompasses. Please don't you make that same mistake; there is much to capture your interest in the cool, green, wooded hills – scenically, architecturally, historically, gastronomically and, as a bonus to all that, there are indeed many super wines to savour at the end of quiet, satisfying days.

One recommendation I am always making to my readers is to order local wines – whatever the region and wherever you are. Identifying them is half the battle – that's one of the objectives my book *French Leave* tries to meet. The reds of this area are amongst my favourite French wines – but it is a white wine from these southern parts of Burgundy that my wife and I remember most; called **Chardonnay**, it's a *varietal* wine, taking its name from the famous grape type used in all the best Burgundy whites. It is particularly potent and we have always been grateful that at the end of our evening meal we have just had a flight of stairs to contend with – rather than a drive home to bed. More often than not it took us all our time to climb those stairs to our waiting bedroom – a real head-spinning wine, believe me. Watch out for it – you'll see it in nearby *Bugey*, too.

I'll start by suggesting you explore the quiet lanes that meander below the rounded hills lining the eastern edge of the area; lanes hemmed in by the hills on one side and the notorious N6, A6 autoroute and River **Saône** on the other. It is in this long strip of country that you will be able to find all the sleepy villages which are a roll-call of Beaujolais wines; **Brouilly**, **Morgon**, **Chiroubles**, **Fleurie**, **Chénas**, **Juliénas** and **St-Amour** amongst them.

The Route de Beaujolais starts on the D43 at **Villefranche-s-Saône** and finishes at **Crêches-s-Saône**, eight kilometres south of **Mâcon**, on the N6. By all means follow the signposted route in its entirety as it winds north – but you must make several *deviations* if you are to enjoy it all the more. First search out the fine, small villages of **Theizé** and **Oingt** – both reward you with super, extensive views. Navigate carefully, climbing up and down until you soon reach the summit called the **Signal de St-Bonnet**. At **Montmelas**, south-east of the summit, you'll see an old château restored by Viollet-le-Duc, the same man who restored the massive La Cité at Carcassonne and the awesome fortress of Pierrefonds, north-east of Paris. You'll come across examples of his work throughout France.

Descend to **Salles** with its ancient priory. Then climb again to **Vaux-en-Beaujolais** – the original *Clochemerle*; there are many other villages, similar in style and spirit, but do be sure not to miss this one. Make the short climb to the summit of **Mont Brouilly**; from its steep sides, a mass of vineyards, comes one of the best of all Beaujolais wines, called **Côte de Brouilly** (*côte* means side).

The 500 year old château at **Corcelles** and the village of **Romanèche-Thorins** (it has a zoo) will reward a detour from the Route de Beaujolais. But most rewarding of all will be the few kilometres it takes to reach the viewpoint called **La Terrasse** – extensive scenes stretch far to the east across the area, on the far side of the Saône, called *Les Dombes*.

What attractions lie to the western side of the long ridge of summits that cap the Beaujolais hills? **Les Echarmeaux** makes a good starting point for you to first head

20   The château at Sercy

south, taking in as many of the *cols* as time allows: the **Col de Favardy** and the **Col de la Croix des Fourches** are two examples. The hills are a mass of woods, cool and tranquil, and a world apart from those murderous ribbons of road down in the Saône Valley. Seek out a valley of quite a different sort – the **Azergues** Valley; there are two ancient villages within its confines that you must certainly explore: **Chamelet** and **Ternand**.

Charlieu should be your next port of call. It is particularly famous for its one thousand year old Bénédictine abbey; and the nearby 15th century cloisters (Cloître des Cordeliers) complement perfectly the solitude of the wooded hills to the east. The town is a gem – full of old architectural treasures. North of Charlieu is a small hilly area called **Le Brionnais** which stretches north to **Paray-le-Monial**. Several tiny villages are dotted throughout Le Brionnais, each with their own fascinating example of Romanesque churches. Your route must take you past two of the best of them: **Semur-en-Brionnais** and **Anzy-le-Duc**. Finish your tour of Le Brionnais at Paray-le-Monial, one of the most important places of pilgrimage in France; the impetus to build the Sacré-Cœur in Paris came from this town. The Romanesque priory church is a replica of nearby **Cluny**.

Before setting off to explore the remaining parts of this area which encircles Cluny, drive south from **Charolles** to **La Clayette** and **Chauffailles**, ensuring you include on your route, when you leave Chauffailles, the narrow D316 that takes you up to the **Montagne de Dun**. All this countryside near Charolles gave its name to the world-famous white cattle called *Charolais*, now seen throughout France. Each of these huge animals can provide as much as a tonne of lean beef.

You'll eat well and cheaply in all these tiny market towns, lost in the hills and away from main tourist routes. I also suggest you revel in their open-air markets; you'll gasp at the fresh local produce and the great variety of it, and you will envy the lucky housewives who can select from the vast array of alternative foods available to them. You'll also be amazed at what good value it all is – picnics will be a treat, I promise you.

The hills and valleys encircling Cluny will recompense whatever amount of time you can set aside to see them. But start with the town itself which – from the 9th to the 12th century – was the spiritual hub of the Christian world. Today, little remains of the Abbey of Cluny which, until the building of St-Peter's in Rome, was the largest Christian church in Europe. Its influence – spiritual, intellectual and artistic – was far-reaching; it radiated from Burgundy, throughout France and into the rest of Europe. Its hundreds of *children* (dependent abbeys and priories) kept alive the Christian faith during periods of history when it came close to dying. Perhaps only your imagination can bring alive the past majesty of the site; but both the small town and the Musée Ochier are interesting enough to warrant a detour and some hours of your time.

West of Cluny are two places of further interest: one is man-made – a château at **Chaumont** with intriguing 17th century stables; the other is a scenic treasure – the **Butte de Suin**, where you'll get extensive views in all directions.

In the valley to the north of Cluny are two modern day phenomena – quite different from each other in their respective ways. At **Taizé** is the Ecumenical community, founded by Brother Roger in 1940, which has attracted tens of

thousands of people, of all nationalities and particularly youngsters, searching for a meaning to their lives. Much of Brother Roger's writings have been translated into English – they are well worth studying.

On the way to Taizé you'll have the chance to see the completely new railway line that has been built from Lyon to Paris to take the TGV (*Train à Grande Vitesse* – very high speed) trains. New stations have been built at Mâcon and Montchanin (north-west of Cluny); they provide you with a chance to try a short fast trip on these 300 kilometres per hour trains of the future.

East of Cluny are several other attractions – you'll have them to yourselves. There are two caves at **Azé** and **Blanot** – the former has water as a feature. Above them is **Mont St-Romain**: the Jura, the Alps, the Saône – all are included in your views. Include the three châteaux at **Berzé-le-Châtel**, **Sercy** and **Cormatin** on your route; it should also take you through the villages of **Chapaize** and **Brancion** – both have interesting churches that are hundreds of years old and the latter has a particularly picturesque example.

To complete your tour of this hilly country, drive south through **Chardonnay** (it gave its name to that grape type I mentioned earlier), **Lugny** and **Vire**; the vineyards surrounding these villages provide their own noble contributions to the fine vintages known as **Côte Mâconnais** wines. The most famous of these comes from the village of **Fuissé** – expensive indeed is that white wine. Near this village is **Solutré** – a prehistoric site lying under a great rock face. Hunters of those days used to drive their quarry over the steep escarpment; vast numbers of animal bones have been found at the base of the cliffs.

LA CLAYETTE

Poste

Simple hotel

A *Logis de France* in the middle of a small market town; it has had a sound reputation for value for money, good cuisine for many decades. You will have seen a great number of the famous white Charolais cattle in the hills around the town; *charolais à la moëlle et au Fleurie* appears on the menu – along with *terrine de saumon, asperges fraîches* and *côtes d'agneau grillées* amongst others.

fpm A–C *meals* NC *rooms* 15 A–C *closed* Mid Dec–mid Jan. Fri evg and Sat (out of season). *post* 71800 La Clayette. S.-et-L. *phone* (85) 28.02.45.

MONTMERLE-SUR-SAONE

Rivage

Comfortable hotel/Terrace

A particularly nice hotel with an attractive site on the east bank of the **Saône** – at the point the bridge crosses the river. An added bonus is a paved, shady terrace with river views. *Petite friture* from the Saône features amongst the specialities – as do *jambon chaud au Porto, grenouilles fraîches à la crème, côte de veau* and *pruneaux Beaujolais.*

fpm A–D *meals* NC *rooms* 18 A–D *closed* Mid–end Sept. Mid Nov–mid Dec. Wed. *post* Montmerle-sur-Saône. 01140 Thoissey. Ain. *phone* (74) 69.33.92.

STE-FOY

Le Brionnais

Simple hotel (no showers or baths)/**Quiet/Terrace**

A modern, isolated building with prices that will suit the smallest of budgets. Charolais beef is offered in various ways – other dishes include *grenouilles, salade à l'huile de noix, andouillette grillée, dodine de canard* and *pâté de grive.* One of the best of the **Le Brionnais** Romanesque churches is at nearby **Semur-en-Brionnais**; be certain not to miss it.

fpm A–B *meals* NC *rooms* 8 A *closed* Feb. Tues evg and Wed midday (except July–Aug). *post* Ste-Foy. 71110 Marcigny. S.-et-L. *phone* (85) 25.83.27.

TAPONAS

Aub. des Sablons

Simple hotel/Quiet/Terrace

A smart *Relais du Silence* and *Logis de France*. It's easy to find, between the autoroute and the River Saône – use the **Belleville** exit. Like the Rivage at **Montmerle** it's handy for *Les Dombes*, too. Menus include a host of interesting dishes: *saucisson cru Lyonnais, sole au beurre, lapin à l'ancienne, fromage blanc à la crème* and *sorbet vigneron.*

fpm A–B *meals* NC *rooms* 15 C *closed* Tues (out of season). *post* Taponas. 69220 Belleville. Rhône. *phone* (74) 66.34.80.

BUGEY

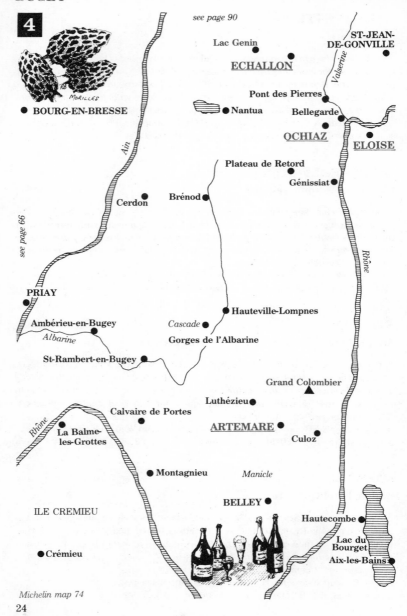

4

MORILLES

● BOURG-EN-BRESSE

see page 90

ST-JEAN-
DE-GONVILLE ●

Lac Genin ●

ECHALLON ●

Valserine

Pont des Pierres ●

● Nantua   Bellegarde ●

OCHIAZ ●

ELOISE

Plateau de Retord ●

Génissiat ●

Ain

Cerdon ●   Brénod ●

see page 99

Rhône

PRIAY ●

Hauteville-Lompnes ●

Ambérieu-en-Bugey ●   *Cascade* ●

Albarine

Gorges de l'Albarine

St-Rambert-en-Bugey ●

Grand Colombier ▲

Luthézieu ●

Calvaire de Portes ●

ARTEMARE ●

Rhône   Culoz ●

La Balme-
les-Grottes ●

● Montagnieu   *Manicle*

BELLEY ●

ILE CREMIEU

Hautecombe ●

Lac du
Bourget

● Crémieu   Aix-les-Bains ●

The countryside of Bugey is the general area that sits in the south-east corner of the *département* of Ain. That *département* is the one that comes first in the alphabetical list of the 95 French *départements*; you will have seen the digits *01* on numerous car number plates and postal codes during your travels in France. It's a corner of that proud land virtually ignored by visitors.

Bugey and *Les Dombes*, together, make up the *département* of Ain; without any shadow of doubt it's also the number one province of France when it comes to measuring the quality and abundance of its culinary skills, treasures and produce. At **Belley**, in 1755, the greatest of all French gastronomes was born, Jean-Anthelme Brillat-Savarin. He was a lawyer by profession, a great linguist, an inventor – the *vaporisateur* (vaporiser) is credited to him – and an excellent violinist; but posterity has remembered him for his legendary book *La Physiologie du gout*, which has influenced so profoundly modern gastronomic thinking ever since. He published it himself, just a few months before his death in 1826. His birthplace in Belley can still be visited – in the Grande Rue. Brillat-Savarin's biographer, Lucien Tendret, another author-lawyer, and, unlike his subject, a talented cook, was also born in this small town; his book *La Table au pays du Brillat-Savarin* is regarded by many as one of the finest books on French regional cooking. Both their names and that of Brillat-Savarin's mother – *La Belle Aurore* – will have been spotted by you at some time or other on French menus.

There is much to see and do in the quiet, wooded hills of Bugey – certainly a few days will give you more than ample opportunity to enjoy it; your evenings will provide you with the chance to enjoy the many culinary pleasures of the *département* – but more of that later.

Have a good look at the south-east corner of Bugey first. Explore Belley: the cathedral; Brillat-Savarin's birthplace; the college where Lamartine was a student; and finally the War Memorial where you'll see the name of one of Brillat-Savarin's distant relatives inscribed on it.

The eastern edge of Bugey is lined by the River **Rhône**. It's not a scenic attraction – far from it – but, nevertheless, it has some interesting industrial aspects worth looking at. Over a century ago two American engineers founded what was then a new industry – the mechanical transport of energy created by hydraulic power over some distance. In their case it was done at **Bellegarde** where the waters of the Rhône and the **Valserine** join; unhappily the cables that carried the current from the energy-creating plant at Bellegarde – at the rate of 20 metres per second – lost 50 per cent of the horsepower that had started out. The project failed as a result. Today however, just south of Bellegarde, you can see one of Europe's largest and most powerful hydro-electric generating stations at **Génissiat**. The dam and whole site is a fine spectacle; it is the first of many schemes along the Rhône that put the river to such effective use on its way to the Mediterranean. Don't miss this engineering marvel.

Once upon a time the Rhône used to flow west at **Culoz** – through the narrow gorge that bisects Bugey; the stream that now flows through the western part is called the **Albarine**. Today, the Rhône continues south at Culoz, makes a loop to the north and then loops again to the south. You'll see huge construction projects south and east of Belley where the waters of the Rhône are being diverted through

Reflections at Lac Genin: a tranquil jewel *hidden* in the pine forests

gigantic channels to create even more electrical power. You'll also see several cement works between Culoz and **St-Rambert-en-Bugey** in the Albarine Valley. 150 years ago Louis Vicat did his first work on the soil of this countryside and it was his discoveries that made it possible for this other new industry – at that time – to establish itself. Apart from the many dams and man-made river channels, you'll also notice the huge new autoroute viaduct near Bellegarde – where, I would imagine, vast amounts of cement have been used in its construction.

North of Culoz there is a viewpoint you must not miss – the **Grand Colombier,** 1525 metres high. The road is steep and narrow; at the summit you'll get extensive views in all directions – you'll see the three lakes of Geneva, Annecy and **Bourget**. You'll also have an eagle's eye view of those man-made sights. Explore all the hills and valleys that make up this southern part of Bugey; the **Gorges de l'Albarine** (with one huge cascade), south-west of **Hauteville-Lompnes**, and the **Calvaire de Portes** are particularly worthwhile diversions.

During your quiet drives in the lanes of these southern hills you'll spot many small vineyards; these provide the grapes that are used for the light white wines of Bugey: **Manicle** is a wine that comes from the general area just north of Belley (it takes its name from that of a rare grape type); **Montagnieu** is a village on the banks of the Rhône that also gives its name to a fine wine. These two wines are recommended ones at the great three star restaurants of Chapel and Blanc in *Les Dombes* – what fame for such obscure, unknown wines!

Across on the eastern banks of the Rhône, as it makes its great semicircle loop around Bugey, lie several other scenic attractions – both man-made and of the natural sort. The Lac du Bourget is one of them; **Aix-les-Bains** is on its eastern shore under the shadow of Mont Revard, which provides one of the best viewpoints in Savoie. Lamartine, who gave his name to that college at Belley, wrote his famous poem about Elvire here. On the opposite bank is the Abbey of **Hautecombe**, a Cistercian abbey, founded by Saint Bernard in 1125.

South of **Ambérieu-en-Bugey**, on the southern bank of the Rhône, are two scenic attractions. The first is the caves of **La Balme-les-Grottes**, where water plays a part in adding to their interest; a few kilometres further south is the old town of **Crémieu**, full of intriguing, ancient buildings – a church, old gates, covered markets and a château are amongst the treasures. Use the lanes that lie between these two differing attractions – terrain called the **Ile Crémieu**.

The northern part of Bugey is a mass of pine-clad hills; the main road from Bellegarde to **Nantua** cuts it in half. Today an ambitious autoroute is being constructed through that same gap in the hills – but, as interesting as that engineering work is, you can ignore the speeding tourists and enjoy the pleasures and delights of the forests. It is all countryside I love dearly; both here, in Bugey, and also as it stretches north into the Jura hills.

To the north of that main road the Valserine Valley provides a thrilling sight: the **Pont des Pierres**; a bridge bestrides the river, which in times of heavy rain is a truly spectacular cascade.

Seek out the tiny **Lac Genin** – an exquisite jewel set amidst the tranquil, wooded hills. It's quite different from the lake which has Nantua at its eastern end; the town has attractive gardens, walks along the lakeside, and offers the chance for boating trips on the lake. Nantua gave its name to the classical crayfish sauce which accompanies *quenelles de brochet Nantua* – dumplings of finely-poached pike. Another speciality in both these hills, and in the Jura further to the north, is the incomparable *poulet aux morilles à la crème* – the perfect example of how the raw materials of the neighbouring countryside can be combined to make a superb dish. The plump white-meat chickens from the Bresse country to the west and the rich dairy cream from the cows who feed so contentedly on the emerald pastures of the nearby hills, combine with one of the best of all the fine edible mushrooms that are found in the same hills – morels.

South of Nantua – in the countryside surrounding **Brénod**, Hauteville and the **Plateau de Retord** – the magnificent *Maquis* of Ain created havoc for the German forces during the Second World War. In 1944 – as you will read in other areas as well – they took a terrible battering from a massive German assault; unhappily, many of the small villages in these secluded hills suffered heavy damage as a result. Explore this totally ignored area and use your imagination to take you back to those days in 1944 – you can quickly grasp, as you can in the *Vercors*, why it made such ideal Resistance country. Then visit the inspiring memorial to all those who lost their lives in the hills – at **Cerdon**.

Nearby are interesting limestone caves and you'll also see vineyards which provide the grapes for excellent *rosé* and sparkling wines; they take the name **Vins du Bugey** – **Cerdon rosé** and **Cerdon** or **Bugey pétillant** (a slight sparkle) and **mousseux** (sparkling). Finally, many other pleasures await you to the west in *Les Dombes* country – of both the scenic and gastronomic sort.

Near Echallon: typical wooded Bugey countryside

ARTEMARE   Vieux Tilleul

Simple hotel/Quiet/Terrace

The hotel has a delectable situation – eight kilometres north of Artemare, at
Luthézieu. There's a lovely shaded terrace and an attractive dining room. Try some
of the local delights like *jambon cru du Savoie, lavaret, omelette aux morilles* and
gratin Dauphinois. Don't miss the really good local wines (from north of Belley)
like **Manicle** and **Chardonnay du Bugey**.
fpm A–D *meals* NC *rooms* 11 B *closed* 1 Jan–mid Feb.
post Luthézieu. 01260 Champagne. Ain. *phone* (79) 87.64.51.

ECHALLON   Aub. de la Semine

Simple restaurant with rooms/Quiet/Terrace/GC

Another real value for money find – with cooking much above average. Dishes
include *terrine Bressane, jambon chaud, poulet à la crème, gratin de queues
d'écrevisses* and *millefeuilles*. Don't under any circumstances miss the exquisite,
tiny **Lac Genin** – only kilometres away to the west; it's ringed by woods and is an
utter delight – you'll not regret the navigation effort finding it.
fpm A–B *meals* NC *rooms* 11 A–B *closed* Mid Oct–end Nov. Sun evg and Mon.
post Echallon. 01490 St-Germain-de-Joux. Ain. *phone* (74) 76.48.75.

ELOISE   Le Fartoret

Comfortable hotel/Secluded/Gardens/Swimming pool/Tennis/Lift

A *Logis de France* and a *Relais du Silence* in a *dead-end* road village, high above the
south bank of the River **Rhône**. It has an extensive list of facilities for guests and it
makes an ideal spot to explore all the country to the east as well. Amongst the
specialities are *jambon cru, entrecôte au poivre vert, crêpe fourée Savoyarde* and
poulet sauté au vinaigre de cidre.
fpm A–C *meals* NC *rooms* 40 C–D *closed* Xmas.
post Eloise. 01200 Bellegarde-sur-Valserine. Ain. *phone* (50) 48.07.18.

OCHIAZ   Aub. de la Fontaine

Comfortable restaurant with rooms/Quiet/Terrace/Gardens

Five kilometres to the west of **Bellegarde** and on the western side of the newly-
opened autoroute; the massive viaduct that carries that road across· the River
Rhône is a spectacular sight – rivalling the Barrage de **Génissiat**. Enjoy *pâté chaud
de canard, omble meunière, turbot Champagne, pintadeau garni, volaille de
Bresse au vinaigre* and *marjolaine Cointreau.*
fpm A–D *meals* C *rooms* 4 B *closed* Jan. Sun evg and Mon.
post Ochiaz. 01200 Bellegarde-sur-Valserine. Ain. *phone* (50)˙48.00.66.

CANTAL – AUBRAC

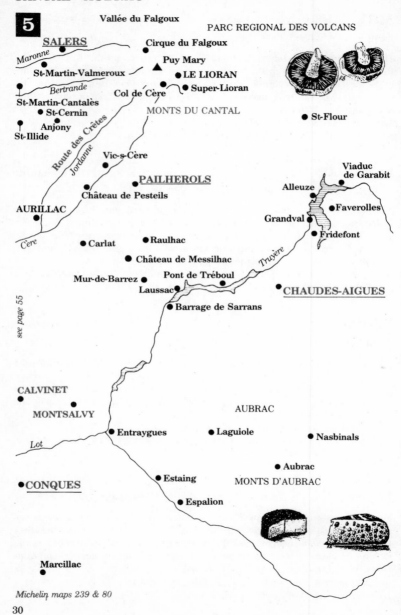

5

Vallée du Falgoux

PARC REGIONAL DES VOLCANS

SALERS

Maronne

Cirque du Falgoux

Puy Mary

St-Martin-Valmeroux

Bertrande

● **LE LIORAN**

Col de Cère

● Super-Lioran

St-Martin-Cantalès

St-Cernin

MONTS DU CANTAL

Anjony

St-Illide

● **St-Flour**

Route des Crêtes

Jordanne

Vic-s-Cère

PAILHEROLS

Viaduc
de Garabit

Château de Pesteils

Alleuze

AURILLAC

Grandval

● **Faverolles**

Cère

● Fridefont

Truyère

Carlat

● Raulhac

Château de Messilhac

Pont de Tréboul

Mur-de-Barrez ●

Laussac

CHAUDES-AIGUES

see page 55

● Barrage de Sarrans

CALVINET

AUBRAC

MONTSALVY

Lot

● Entraygues

● Laguiole

● Nasbinals

● Aubrac

● **CONQUES**

● Estaing

MONTS D'AUBRAC

● Espalion

Marcillac

Michelin maps 239 & 80

The official Government boundaries of Auvergne stretch from Moulins – far to the north in Bourbonnais country – to the banks of the infant River Lot in the south. The southern half of this huge piece of countryside is the Massif Central: it is a mass of mountain country, much of it being dominated by the peaks of extinct volcanoes – known as *puys*; all of them lie in a glorious Regional Nature Park which has a fascinating name – **Parc Régional des Volcans**.

My chosen area is the southernmost part of Auvergne: the name of Cantal – Aubrac derives from the **Monts du Cantal** – the various *puys* of Cantal which are at the southern end of the regional park; and to the south-east, the mountainous region of **Aubrac**, which is the countryside between the River **Truyère** and the River Lot. For good measure I trespass across the banks of the Lot and include at least one of the most glorious of French treasures. Cantal – Aubrac is superb country; it is much the most ignored part of Auvergne. The equally appealing terrain circling the town of Clermont-Ferrand is not one of my *hidden* areas; I love it, but like the Dordogne, it can be a very busy tourist centre. My choice here is one of the quietest parts of France – full of mountains, woods, green pastures, splendid river valleys and old historical towns. This is yet another area where the more you get off the beaten track, the more you will enjoy yourself; and where a map will repay its small outlay a thousand times over – I seem to repeat that observation very frequently through the pages of this book. Immerse yourself in maps – pore over them; every hour spent studying a good, well-designed, large-scale map will be time wisely spent. Become a *Francophiliac Mapoholic*!

I'll start by telling you something about Cantal – all the country to the north of the River Truyère. The peaks of the Monts du Cantal dominate the scene between Salers and **St-Flour**. Indeed, Salers makes an ideal starting point to explore the whole area; it's also perfectly situated for you to head north-west into another of my hidden areas – *Corrèze*. It is hard to say what I like most about tiny ancient Salers: I think I would put its fantastic site first, sitting on a basalt plateau high above the **Maronne** Valley; then its narrow, old streets, full of interesting, handsome houses – particularly the turreted splendours lining the Grande-Place; the views from the Esplanade de Barrouze; and finally, its centuries-old church. It's a magnificent *hors d'œuvre* before you start the next series of appetising courses that await you as you head south.

I meant that phrase in two senses – the scenic specialities and the gastronomic ones. Consider the latter first: there's a cheese called **Cantal** – often called **Fourme de Salers** – which is made in these hills and is considered to be the oldest of all French cheeses, its origins going back over 2,000 years; it was praised by Pliny. It's a semi-hard cow's milk cheese with a nutty flavour. The word *fourme* used to describe how the herdsmen shaped and formed the milk curd to make their cheeses. The verdant mountain pastures are perfect for the cows.

Scenic specialities abound in the vicinity of Salers. Downstream there are a series of charming little roads straddling the Maronne and **Bertrande** Valleys – bonuses are the ancient village churches of **St-Martin-Valmeroux, St-Martin-Cantalès, St-Illide** and **St-Cernin**. Just east of the latter is the 15th century castle of **Anjony**; a super site adds extra pleasure to a splendid-looking building and its interior treasures of tapestries and wall paintings.

31

Salers: the Grande-Place

When you have feasted on all these pleasures travel east along the D680 towards the **Puy Mary** – a superb mountain drive. Make the *deviation* north to the **Vallée du Falgoux** if time allows, but the principal interest of the D680 run is the final climb up the sides of the **Cirque du Falgoux** (*cirque* means *amphitheatre* of mountains in this case) to a pass just below the Puy Mary. Intoxicating views will be your reward if you head south along the **Route des Crêtes** – one of the best mountain drives in the Massif Central. But be careful with your navigating – it's vital you use the D35 road that runs along the ridge of peaks that line the northern side of the **Jordanne** Valley.

Aurillac will be the terminus on this drive; interesting enough with its abbey church, a museum and some old houses – but my preferred choice would be to double back up the River **Cère** to its source. Just before **Vic-s-Cère** is the **Château de Pesteils**, overlooking the valley – its attractions are its dungeons, tapestries and frescoes. Explore Vic and then, before continuing upstream, climb a few kilometres to the east for views of the whole valley. Near the source of the Cère don't make the mistake of using the tunnel that cuts under the **Col de Cère**; instead, climb up through the pine forests to **Super-Lioran** – invigorating country with tremendous views of Puy Mary to the west.

Make St-Flour your next port of call. It sits on a table of basalt high above the surrounding countryside. The town has always had great strategic importance – no wonder when you consider its site: a Gothic cathedral, narrow streets lined with centuries-old buildings, and extensive views from its ramparts are amongst the treats in store for you. Other treats to please your palate include delicious examples of the Auvergne *charcuterie: jambons crus* (raw mountain hams); *saucissons* and *saucisses sèches* (dried sausages) of all sorts; pork *pâtés*; and *friand Sanflorin* (pork meat and herbs in a pastry case).

Now allow time to explore one of the unknown rivers of France, the Truyère. Make your first sight of it south-east of St-Flour from the N9. The river view is memorable enough but a man-made scenic splendour that will share your interest is the **Viaduc de Garabit**. This astonishing railway bridge was designed by Boyer and built by Eiffel (who conceived the Eiffel Tower in Paris). The river has been made to work by the construction of a dam at **Grandval**. No roads line the banks of the man-made lake; nevertheless, the D13 is an interesting road that takes you through **Faverolles** and **Fridefont** – detour north to the splendid château ruins at **Alleuze**. Then on to **Chaudes-Aigues** – this place is unusual in that it gets its hot water (also used for central heating) from natural springs.

To the west the road descends to the **Pont de Tréboul**, where you cross a narrow man-made lake. Include the pretty setting of **Laussac** on your route and continue on to the huge **Barrage de Sarrans** at the end of the lake – a really formidable piece of engineering and architectural brilliance. Now detour north into the hills again to attractive **Mur-de-Barrez** and then on to tiny **Raulhac** (both providing marvellous views) – passing on your way the medieval **Château de Messilhac**, lost to the west of the D600. If time allows detour west to **Carlat**, where you'll have extensive views of the Cère Valley once more.

After enjoying all this scenic wonderland I implore you to do two things. First see as much as you can of the hills to both east and west of **Montsalvy**: as I write these

33

words I can visualise the handsome trees of that quiet, charming countryside – trees which are at their best in May, June, September and October. Then use the D601 – 15 kilometres to the west of Montsalvy – to descend to the River Lot and climb again to fabulous Conques.

Conques is an enchanting village – lost in the hills south of the Lot. The Romanesque church is remarkable – its *treasure*, even more so. Sainte Foy was a young Christian martyr; her relics were at Agen, where they worked miracles. Legend has it that a monk from Conques worked faithfully at Agen for 10 years, then removed the relics to Conques, where they have since remained.

Then retrace your steps back to the Lot and follow it upstream to **Entraygues** where a fine Gothic bridge graces this old pilgrimage stopping place. Continue up the Lot to **Estaing** and **Espalion**; the Lot is at its best in these stretches. Estaing is dominated by its castle – Espalion by its 13th century bridge and castle. Enjoy the local wines hereabouts – the **Vin d'Entraygues et du Fel**, **Vin d'Estaing** and the **Marcillac** wines (they go well with the Auvergne cheeses).

Finally, all that remains are the hills to the north of the Lot Valley – the **Monts d'Aubrac**. I can't truthfully say that this mountain area is scenically captivating. The whole area is a massive pasture – hardly inhabited by man but certainly dominated by cattle. In late spring those pastures are a blanket of colour – wild flowers everywhere. The towns of **Aubrac**, **Nasbinals** and **Laguiole** are important centres for cattle – particularly the latter two which are famous for their fairs. **Laguiole** is also renowned for its cheese – similar to **Cantal**; be certain to try the cheese with those local wines described earlier.

34

CHAUDES-AIGUES

Aux Bouillons d'Or

Comfortable restaurant with rooms/Lift/GC

This is the town with the hottest spa waters in Europe – 82 degrees C. A modernised, tall, narrow building with five floors – don't worry, there's a lift. Much above average standard of cuisine as the chef has a sound training pedigree. *Filet de truite au blanc de poireaux, tourte au Cantal, gratin de queues d'écrevisses* and *grand dessert* are just some of the mouth-watering specialities.
fpm A–D *meals* NC *rooms* 12 C *closed* Dec–Feb. Tues (mid Oct–end Apl).
post 15110 Chaudes-Aigues. Cantal. *phone* (71) 23.51.42.

CONQUES

Ste-Foy

Comfortable hotel/Quiet

An utter gem of a place, creeper-covered and nestling in the shadow of one of France's true jewels – the Eglise Ste-Foy. You'll fall in love with this exquisite village with its priceless site; to the immediate north is the bonus of the Lot Valley. Dinner only here and just one menu. Basic it is with things like *tarte Auvergnate*, Auvergne cheeses such as **Cantal** and **Cahors** wines.
fpm A *meals* NC *rooms* 20 B–E *closed* Mid Oct – Mar.
post Conques. 12320 St-Cyprien-sur-Dourdou. Aveyron. *phone* (65) 69.84.03.

PAILHEROLS

Aub. des Montagnes

Simple hotel/Quiet/Terrace

A shining example of what value for money can really mean: 5 simple courses for 35 francs! The dish of cheeses offered (left for you to help yourself) puts many more famous and pretentious places to shame. Everything is freshly cooked and the chances are you won't be given a menu – but don't let that stop you enjoying the Auvergne dishes. A simple *Logis* over 1000 metres above sea-level.
fpm A *meals* NC *rooms* 11 A *closed* Oct–Feb.
post Pailherols. 15800 Vic-sur-Cère. Cantal. *phone* (71) 47.57.01.

SALERS

Le Bailliage

Comfortable hotel/Quiet/Gardens

Don't be put off by the petrol pumps in front of this modern place. In no way will they prevent you enjoying the hotel, the ancient town of Salers, the varied countryside that lies in all directions and the excellent reputation Charles Bancarel has for his cooking skills: amongst local dishes he serves are *jambon de montagne, Auvergne charcuterie* and *tripoux.*
fpm A *meals* C *rooms* 30 A–C *closed* Mid Nov–mid Dec.
post 15410 Salers. Cantal. *phone* (71) 40.71.95.

CEVENNES

6

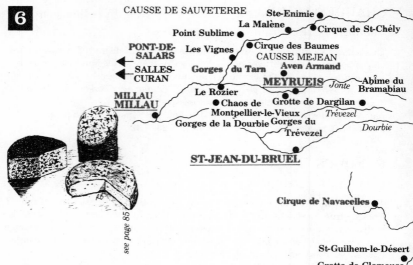

CAUSSE DE SAUVETERRE   Ste-Enimie ●

La Malène ●

Point Sublime ●   ● Cirque de St-Chély

PONT-DE-SALARS   Les Vignes   ● Cirque des Baumes

SALLES-CURAN   Gorges / du Tarn   CAUSSE MEJEAN

Aven Armand

MILLAU   Le Rozier   MEYRUEIS   *Jonte*   Abîme du Bramabiau

MILLAU   ● Chaos de   Grotte de Dargilan ●

Montpellier-le-Vieux   *Trévezel*

Gorges de la Dourbie   Gorges du

Trévezel   *Dourbie*

ST-JEAN-DU-BRUEL

Cirque de Navacelles ●

St-Guilhem-le-Désert

Grotte de Clamouse

Lac du Salagou

Mourèze ●   Gignac

see page 85

see page 85

Michelin maps 80 & 83

Nature has endowed the mountainous area of the Cévennes with a glorious legacy – nowhere else in France do spectacular sights come so thick and fast. Many of them are underground – fantastic grottoes and caves; others are carved, tortuous valleys and gorges; some are rugged mountain cliffs – their summits offer a variety of panoramic views. Few man-made treasures are to be found in this often desolate landscape; this will come as no surprise as the high plateaux – called *causses* – are barren, boulder-strewn places. Here Mother Nature has not painted the countryside with green landscapes – her handiwork is of a more violent kind and you must search diligently to find it. Maps are a must.

Much the most famous of these attractions is the River **Tarn**; it's one of the great natural wonders of Western Europe and the **Gorges du Tarn** are indeed the first and most important sight you should seek out. The river has carved out a dramatic deep gorge in the limestone hills; a relatively short distance of 35 kilometres separates the two villages of **Ste-Enimie** and **Le Rozier** and it's the valley between these two spots that is the most breathtaking. Put aside plenty of time to follow the narrow road alongside the river's northern bank on this stretch.

Ste-Enimie is an attractive, ancient riverside town – seen at its best from the roads high above it that then drop, in precipitous fashion, to the Tarn. A few kilometres downstream you'll pass the Château de la Caze – nowadays a luxury hotel. From **La Malène** you can make boat trips – an even better way to both see and enjoy the river's stunning treasures that await you downstream: the first is Les Détroits; followed shortly by the **Cirque des Baumes**, which is at the point the torrent takes a 90 degrees turn to the south. The rock faces on these sections are

36

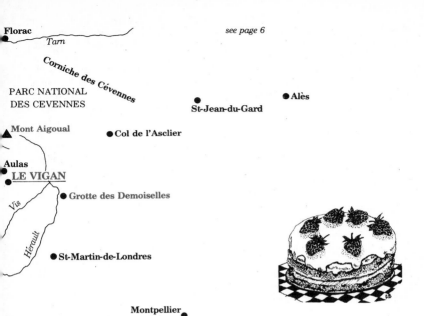

Florac

Tarn

see page 6

Corniche des Cévennes

PARC NATIONAL
DES CEVENNES

● **Alès**

● **St-Jean-du-Gard**

▲ **Mont Aigoual**

● **Col de l'Asclier**

Aulas
● **LE VIGAN**

Vis

● **Grotte des Demoiselles**

Hérault

● **St-Martin-de-Londres**

Montpellier●

beautifully coloured – orange, sand and shades of grey and brown.

As important as it is to see the river from its banks, it is just as vital that you also view it from points above the deep gorge. Leave Ste-Enimie to the south – the D986 – and climb high to the first viewpoint at the **Cirque de St-Chély**. Continue on, first making a detour to the point where the narrow road falls away below you to La Malène; then, again, make a *deviation* to the Roc des Hourtous – the view from there *merits a detour* say Michelin. But the greatest view of all is the one from the **Point Sublime** – above the northern cliffs of the Cirque des Baumes; cross the river at **Les Vignes** and climb the steep lanes that take you to this magnificent and breathtaking viewpoint.

The limestone plateau to the north of the Tarn is the **Causse de Sauveterre**; the one to the south is the **Causse Méjean**. The latter has on its southern flanks some more superb country – and, for good measure, hides under its rock-covered surface one of the greatest caves in France. The river **Jonte** joins the Tarn at Le Rozier; from that junction follow the wooded riverside road that runs alongside this fine example of the astonishing carvings that water can make – over thousands of centuries – upon limestone rocks. **Meyrueis** is the first small town of any significance that you'll reach; it's attractively situated and has, within its neighbourhood, both the exceptional cave mentioned earlier – the **Aven Armand**, north of the Jonte – and, due south, on the opposite side of the same river, the cave called the **Grotte de Dargilan**.

Aven Armand is an amazing, floodlit underground hall; truly a petrified forest – the Forêt Vierge. It was discovered as recently as 1897 and it contains within its

37

deep underground cave some fantastic stalagmites. The Grotte de Dargilan is a series of smaller caves full of stalagmites and stalactites – its entrance is in the rock face high above the River Jonte.

A third river valley in the northern half of this area now clamours for your attention – the **Dourbie**, another tributary of the Tarn, which it joins at **Millau**. I wrote in *French Leave* that spectacles come thick and fast on this run – take lots of spare film to capture all the stunning sights. The **Gorges de la Dourbie** are exciting enough, but other natural wonders also merit your time. The strangely-named **Chaos de Montpellier-le-Vieux** is the first of them – vast numbers of strange, huge rock formations litter the ground; the site sits high above the northern cliffs of the Dourbie. Immediately to the north of the Gorges de la Dourbie is the smaller **Gorges du Trévezel**. By following the River **Trévezel** you'll enter the **Parc National des Cévennes**, full of high wooded hills and interlaced by deserted, thrilling roads. It's renowned for its flora and fauna; but before you do justice to this quieter, less flamboyant aspect of Nature's legacy hereabouts, one further underground attraction has to be sought out – the **Abîme du Bramabiau**. It's a subterranean river, small *cirque* and caves – all in one.

The highest point of the National Park is **Mont Aigoual** – from the observatory (1567 metres) you will get glorious and extensive views in all directions. To the north-east, as far as the extremities of my map, you'll see some of the hills that hide a whole series of narrow, twisty lanes – unknown by tourists and consequently virtually unused. One magnificent scenic spectacular is better known – the **Corniche des Cévennes**; it runs, via the D9, across a mass of deserted country, from

Gorges du Tarn: near La Malène

Florac to **St-Jean-du-Gard**, a distance of 53 kilometres.

From St-Jean-du-Gard head south-west once more to **Le Vigan**, across the minor **Col de l'Asclier** – wild country, magnificent views and solitude will be your reward. South of Le Vigan you'll notice clear signs that you have reached the south – vines and olive trees begin to appear. But before we turn our attention to the River **Hérault** – you'll see it for the first time when you descend the Col de l'Asclier – head further south-west from Le Vigan to the first of three more really superb three-star curiosities of nature.

Navigate carefully on Michelin map 80 to the Cirque de Navacelles. *Cirque* means *amphitheatre* of mountains or hills; in this case perhaps the most unusual of the *cirques* that abound throughout France. Various streams and underground springs join together shortly before the *cirque* to form, at Navacelles, the most extraordinary sight – a *cirque* surrounding the loops of the river far below. To top it all there's a magnificent cascade as well. Double back to follow the **Vis** downstream, through its gorges, until it joins the Hérault. Unlike the Tarn and its many tributaries, the Hérault flows into the Mediterranean – the countryside you have been enjoying is the watershed between the Mediterranean and the Atlantic.

The third essential detour is near to this junction of the Vis and Hérault – the Grotte des Demoiselles. A funicular takes you to the entrance of the vast hall – it is over 50 metres high and full of breathtaking examples of stalagmites and stalactites. The great dry cavern hides in its depths a fascinating formation – the stalagmite called The Virgin and Child – for all the world like a man-made statue. The terrain here changes its character completely in a few kilometres.

For much of the River Hérault's next stretch of its journey south towards the Mediterranean it has the countryside to itself – no roads hug its banks. Two ancient villages should be included on your route downstream: **St-Martin-de-Londres** and **St-Guilhem-le-Désert** both have ecclesiastical treasures – the abbey church at the latter is especially interesting. Three kilometres to the south is yet another marvellous cave, the **Grotte de Clamouse**; weird and unusual formations line the floor and ceilings of these caves and, apart from their really curious shape, some of the stalactites are unusually coloured as well.

By **Gignac**, the Hérault has entered the flat strip of land that follows the curve of the Mediterranean – called Bas Languedoc. You will be well aware now that you are entering a mass of wine-producing country. Much of the wine from Languedoc is pretty tasteless stuff but, in the neighbourhood of Gignac, you'll find some excellent examples of the better Languedoc wines. North-west of the town are two villages with a good reputation for their red wines: St-Saturnin and Montpeyroux. Most of the grapes grown in these vast vineyards yield red wine; north-east of **Montpellier**, the Clairette grape is used to make dry white wines. The heady, sweet dessert wine – **Muscat de Frontignan** – comes from the area immediately to the south of Montpellier and alongside the huge Thau lake; the latter is highly reputed for its large mussels and good-quality oysters.

The final scenic attraction that merits a detour is the Cirque de Mourèze; another world of amazingly-shaped rock formations similar to those at the Chaos de Montpellier-le-Vieux. The *cirque* surrounds the small village of **Mourèze**, south of the man-made **Lac du Salagou**.

40   Cirque de Navacelles: a magnificent view from the northern approach road

MEYRUEIS Grand Hôtel Europe

Comfortable hotel/Gardens/Swimming pool/Lift

The gardens and pool are at an annexe 200 metres up the road – the Hôtel du Mont Aigoual. Both buildings are smart, modern places and the small town is perfectly placed for endless trips; but first relish the pines of the high Cévennes to the southeast – don't bypass the **Abîme du Bramabiau** – and then under no circumstances miss the underground treats at **Aven Armand** and the **Grotte de Dargilan**.
fpm A *meals* C *rooms* 50 A–B *closed* Oct-Mar.
post 48150 Meyrueis. Lozère. *phone* (66) 45.60.05.

MILLAU Château de Creissels

Comfortable hotel/Secluded/Gardens

A charming place two kilometres from Millau on the D992 St-Affrique road. It's a modern hotel with a new extension added to an old château, only parts of which still stand – particularly picturesque is a splendid tower; a medieval church is just yards from the entrance. Sound cuisine like *truite au vert de poireaux* and *feuilleté au Roquefort*; the bonus is the attractive, tranquil site.
fpm A–B *meals* C *rooms* 30 B–D *closed* Mid Dec–end Jan. Wed (out of season).
post 12100 Millau. Aveyron. *phone* (65) 60.16.59.

ST-JEAN-DU-BRUEL Midi

Simple hotel/Quiet

A simple *Logis de France* it may be but it has a quiet, attractive site on the south bank of the River **Dourbie** and an ever-increasing reputation for value for money cuisine. Great use is made of the local raw materials – witness the following: *truites, omelette au Roquefort, omelette aux cèpes, champignons des Causses, confit de canard* and many, many more.
fpm A–B *meals* C *rooms* 18 A–B *closed* Mid Nov–mid Mar.
post St-Jean-du-Bruel. 12230 La Cavalerie. Aveyron. *phone* (65) 62.26.04.

LE VIGAN Mas Quayrol

Comfortable hotel/Secluded

A delightful spot high above and to the north of the village of **Aulas**, which itself is seven kilometres from Le Vigan towards **Mont Aigoual**. It's a real sun trap facing south; the bedrooms are in a modern separate building. I implore you not to miss the **Cirque de Navacelles** to the south. Cuisine is basic with local produce like *champignons, truites,* smoked meats and **pélardon** (goat's milk cheese).
fpm A–B *meals* NC *rooms* 16 C–D *closed* Oct–Apl.
post Aulas. 30120 Le Vigan. Gard. *phone* (66) 91.12.38.

CHAINE DES ARAVIS

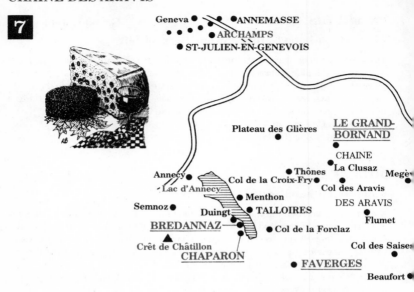

7

Michelin map 74

This small area – the **Chaîne des Aravis** – is centred on the high mountains between **Lac d' Annecy** to the west and the even higher peaks of the **Chaîne du Mont Blanc** to the east. I'll be suggesting you seek out sights that are hidden in this mass of glorious mountain country; you'll not be able to cover ground rapidly, as roads tend to snake first up, and then down the steep slopes – but bear in mind that a circle with a 60 kilometre radius, drawn with the **Col des Aravis** at its centre, encompasses all the terrain shown on the accompanying map.

The Alps have always been like a magnet for me; no wonder, as the first ten years of my life were spent in the high Himalayas. My aim is to persuade you to spend a few days in these inspiring mountains – and encourage you to leave the few main roads that bisect them and explore instead the minor tracks that will lead you to the real Haute-Savoie.

Lake Annecy is the most beautiful of all French lakes. To see both the lake and the hills at their best, make two separate drives. The first will take you up the D41 that runs due south from the town of **Annecy**; it climbs up through thick pine forests to the summit called the **Crêt de Châtillon** on the **Semnoz** mountain. If you have been fortunate enough to choose a clear day – try to leave it until late afternoon, when the sun is in the west – you will get an exceptional view of the lake below you, the hills that form a shapely backdrop on its eastern shore and, far to the east, the majestic dome of **Mont Blanc**.

Now enjoy the eastern bank of the lake at your leisure; but do it this way. First use the narrow road, the D42, that climbs up to the **Col de la Forclaz**, high above the lake. On your descent, as you travel north, stop at the tiny Ermitage de St-Germain.

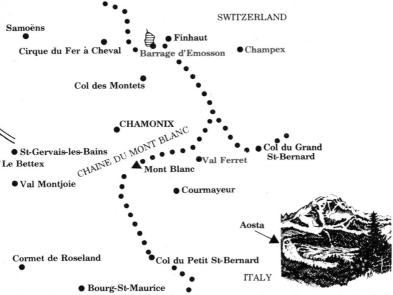

Samoëns

Cirque du Fer à Cheval

Finhaut

Barrage d'Emosson

SWITZERLAND

Champex

Col des Montets

CHAMONIX

St-Gervais-les-Bains

Le Bettex

CHAINE DU MONT BLANC

Val Ferret

Col du Grand St-Bernard

Mont Blanc

Val Montjoie

Courmayeur

Aosta

Cormet de Roseland

Col du Petit St-Bernard

ITALY

Bourg-St-Maurice

This 11th century Bénédictine Saint returned here after a pilgrimage to the Holy Land; earlier, he had founded the monastery at nearby **Talloires**, far below and nestling like a jewel alongside Lake Annecy. That monastery is now a luxurious hotel – the Abbaye.

Another Saint – Bernard de Menthon – was born in the nearby château at **Menthon**; he was overshadowed by his namesake, the great St-Bernard of Clairvaux, Cluny and Cîteaux. St-Bernard of Menthon was born in the 10th century; the present building was rebuilt 400 years ago. It was St-Bernard of Menthon who was the founder of the hospices on the **Col du Grand St-Bernard** and the **Col du Petit St-Bernard** – more about those two high passes later.

Finally, descend to Talloires – there is no prettier lakeside spot in France. Lac d'Annecy, together with its near neighbours, Lac du Bourget and Lac Léman, yield *piscatorial treasures* unknown anywhere else in France. The menus of many local restaurants are built around these superb fish: salmon trout, some a metre long and weighing 15 kilograms; *omble chevalier*, the most subtle and finest-tasting of all freshwater fish (a char – it looks like a salmon trout); *féra*; *lavaret*; *brochet* and *lotte* (a burbot, not unlike an eel).

The hills and valleys to the east of Lake Annecy were one of the most important areas for those brave members of the Resistance movement during the Second World War. The *Maquisards* of Haute-Savoie caused significant problems for the Germans – equipment was parachuted to them on the **Plateau des Glières**, a few kilometres to the north of **Thônes**. Over 400 of them were killed in those hills during early 1944. Three kilometres to the west of Thônes, on the D909, is a cemetery

43

where most of them are buried. Find the time to pay homage to the patriots of the *Maquis* – a small museum lies alongside the cemetery. Acting as sentinels are two cascades – appropriately bringing water down from the Glières Plateau.

In the verdant pastures surrounding busy Thônes you'll hear cowbells clanging away – ringing loudly to remind you that the handsome cows they adorn are the providers of the famous cheese – **Reblochon**. A local term – *reblocher* – means 'to milk the cow for the second time'. This rich milking produces an excellent, gold-coloured, small flat disk of cheese; stop at the farms where you see the sign – *Reblochon vente ici* – and buy some. In the spring and during the early summer you'll be thrilled by the glorious Alpine flowers that grow in these same green pastures, amongst the best to be found in the entire Alps.

All the roads hereabouts leading up to the *cols* are rewarding drives; particularly so are the **Col de la Croix-Fry** and the Col des Aravis. At **Flumet**, continue due south up the **Col des Saises** – all magnificent country and, as a bonus, you'll have it to yourselves. Descend into the village of **Beaufort** – the home of another famous Savoie cheese. This cheese, together with **Emmental**, from the countryside just north of Annecy, is made at *fruitières* – cooperative processing plants. The word is a derivation of the Latin *fructus*, meaning yield or production. Both are pressed, cooked cheeses – like **Gruyère**; **Beaufort** has no holes; **Emmental** has them, the size of walnuts. *Fondue* in these mountains features **Beaufort** cheese and the dry white wine from **Apremont** (see the chapter called *Chartreuse*).

The cheeses that abound in the mountain areas (in Savoie, in the Jura and in the Massif Central) are, for the most part, of the hard or semi-hard variety, invariably

The southern climb of the Col des Aravis

made from cow's milk. In other parts of France you'll be offered all sorts of cheeses; made from the milk of cows (*vaches*), goats (*chèvres*) or ewes (*brebis*). Many will be soft and runny and some will look anything but appetising. But don't be prejudiced about them and don't turn your nose up at them as I used to 25 years ago. Thankfully, it didn't take me too many years to discover what I had missed. **Fromage blanc** is one example; it doesn't always look too appetising, but if you have never sampled this fresh cream cheese, eaten with sugar and fresh cream, you've missed one of life's pleasures.

If you want to explore some of the greatest of high passes continue east from Beaufort along the D217 and the D902; the latter is a new road climbing the **Cormet de Roseland** and is the first major pass. A descent into **Bourg-St-Maurice** is followed by another pass that climbs up through a series of zigzag bends to the summit of the Col du Petit St-Bernard. To the north are majestic views of Mont Blanc. You descend into Italy and two options await you in the **Aosta** Valley: you can continue your high passes tour by driving east and then north to the Col du Grand St-Bernard – be sure to make the short *deviation* up to **Champex**, the prettiest of all small Alpine lakes; or, you can take the alternative drive through the engineering marvel of the Mont Blanc tunnel. Whatever you do, spare time to explore the *dead-end* **Val Ferret**, north-east of **Courmayeur**; it's a lovely unspoilt valley.

The mass of mountains to the north of **Chamonix** hide several amazing sights – created both by Nature and man. From **Finhaut** (just across the Swiss border) an excellent new road takes you up to the staggering **Barrage (Dam) d'Emosson**. What amazing views to the east and south await you. On your way there stop for an hour or so at the summit of the **Col des Montets** and walk the easy, sign-posted path that features so many varieties of Alpine flowers and plants; this fascinating, tiny bit of mountain country is called La Réserve des Aiguilles Rouges.

The mountain wall that forms the backdrop to the western side of Lac d'Emosson gives no indication of what hides on the other side – the **Cirque du Fer à Cheval**. The only way you can reach this astonishing *amphitheatre* of mountains is by driving east from **Samoëns**; in the late spring dozens of cascades shoot forth the melted snows from the glaciers and snowfields high above you. Another *dead-end* valley, ignored by so many, is the **Val Montjoie**; it runs due south from the spa town of **St-Gervais-les-Bains**. Above it, on the hills to the west, are tiny lanes that take you up to **Le Bettex**; a clear day will reward you with the awesome spectacle of Mont Blanc, sitting like a sleeping giant across the valley.

Much of the countryside I have described in these few pages you'll have to yourselves – but if you wish to enjoy many of the other pleasures of the mountain country encircling the Chaîne des Aravis, you must share them with numerous other tourists. What are these attractions? There is picturesque Annecy, with its arcaded, pedestrian-only streets, its charming river and gardens bordering the priceless lake; and the resorts of Chamonix, St-Gervais and **Megève** provide you with many opportunities to take cable-cars or rack-railways to the summits of several high peaks. Sadly, these trips cost money. Try one or two of them; but I am prepared to bet that my philosophy of getting away from the few busy main roads will reward you far more richly and will leave indelible memories in your subconscious mind – to be recalled and treasured in the years to come.

Col des Montets: the walk through La Réserve des Aiguilles Rouges

BREDANNAZ   Azur du Lac
Simple hotel/Terrace/Gardens

The hotel is between the road and Lake Annecy; bedrooms overlooking the lake will
be quieter and will have lovely views – they will also be more expensive. Boating
and bathing facilities are on hand in the hotel gardens – as are games for children.
Enjoy *friture* and *filet de perche* from the lake – and also dishes like *coquelet rôti*
and *entrecôte maître d'hôtel*. Try the **Savoie** wines.
fpm A–B *meals* C *rooms* 30 A–D *closed* Oct–Feb.
post Brédannaz. 74210 Faverges. H.-Savoie. *phone* (50) 68.67.49.

CHAPARON   Châtaigneraie
Simple hotel/Secluded/Gardens

This is the place for those of you who want utter peace and quiet at all costs – seek
out this charming *Logis de France* with its large, shaded *garden* (in reality a small,
green field). It's south of Brédannaz and a kilometre or two from the lake. Pretty
obviously, fish features strongly in the cuisine – *petite friture, omble chevalier* and
truites (prepared in various ways).
fpm A–D *meals* NC *rooms* 21 C–D *closed* Nov–Dec. Mon (Oct–Easter).
post Chaparon. 74210 Faverges. H.-Savoie. *phone* (50) 44.30.67.

FAVERGES   Alpes
Simple hotel

A small *Logis* away from the main road; small it may be but it has a sound reputation
for good cuisine. Enjoy *gateau de lapereau, truite au Riesling* and *tartes* of various
kinds. But if it's real peace and quiet you want with lovely views try the Gay Séjour,
four km. to the south – praised by a *French Leave* reader (I got the tip *after* my
research trips, but I'll be there soon). Try Tamié – a local monastery cheese.
fpm A–D *meals* NC *rooms* 20 A–D *closed* Nov–mid Dec. Mon (except rest. in July–
Aug). *post* P1. Gambetta. 74210 Faverges. H.-Savoie. *phone* (50) 44.50.0.5.

LE GRAND-BORNAND   La Joyère
Comfortable hotel/Quiet/Terrace/Swimming pool/Lift

A large chalet-style building high above and to the east of the village, which is so
much nicer than nearby **La Clusaz**. The cuisine is pretty basic stuff with offerings
like *jambon de montagne* and *truite aux amandes*. But this may be the opportunity
for you to spend a few extra francs on mouthwatering local specialities like *raclette*
and *fondue Savoyarde*.
fpm A–B *meals* NC *rooms* 35 D *closed* Mid Sept–mid Dec. Easter–mid June.
post 74450 Le Grand-Bornand. H.-Savoie. *phone* (50) 67.42.66.
Stop Press: Hotel now closed – use Gay Séjour at Faverges (see above).

CHARTREUSE

8

Chambéry

Chignin

Les Charmettes

Montmélian

Lac d'Aiguebelette

Apremont

Abîmes

Col du Granier

▲ Mont Granier

Lac de Paladru

La Rochette

Grottes des Echelles

Gorges du Bréda

Guiers Vif

Les Echelles

Pontcharra

St-Pierre-d'Entremont

MASSIF DE LA CHARTREUSE

St-Laurent-du-Pont

Col du Cucheron

Couvent de la Grande Chartreuse

Guiers Mort

▲ La Scia

Voiron

ST-PIERRE-DE-CHARTREUSE
ST-PIERRE-DE-CHARTREUSE

COL DE
LA PLACETTE

Col de la Charmette

▲ Charmant Som

Voreppe

COL DE PORTE

Ténaison

Isère

see page 144

Lancey

Grenoble

URIAGE

▲ Croix de Chamrousse

BRESSON

Chamrousse
BRIE-ET-ANGONNES

Michelin maps 74 & 77

It is less than 60 kilometres from **Chambéry** to **Grenoble**; the newly-built autoroute offers you the opportunity to cover that short distance in little over 30 minutes – if you so wish. The vast majority of travellers in this corner of France seize the chance; they blast up and down the main roads and autoroutes that line the dull and ugly River **Isère** – highways that both lead to, and connect, the two towns. A small number of fortunate travellers, who are in the know, and who plan their holiday itineraries carefully, are the beneficiaries of their fellow motorists' relentless desire for speed at all costs.

The wise traveller puts aside the right amount of time – perhaps just one day, maybe longer – to climb high above the Isère into the entrancing, secretive mountains of the **Massif de la Chartreuse**.

It has been my great fortune to use the few roads that cross the Massif during every season of the year. My first visit was in the month of January, more than 20 years ago; I was reconnoitring – for rallying – the narrow D912 and D512 roads that snake up and down the **Col du Granier** and the **Col de Porte**. Deep snow lay everywhere; most of the route was ice bound and required great care. It was a hectic and busy time, driving the narrow lanes and making rally notes for future reference; nevertheless, a magnetic fascination for those appealing peaks, forests and valleys took a grip – and it wasn't long before I returned. There is no other corner of France that I love more – it has drawn me back year after year with a special fascination which I find hard to analyse.

In spring I've seen the roaring streams full of ice-cold, milky-white water. The woods have been ablaze with the first tints of spring green and the pastures blanketed with wild flowers. In high summer my family have enjoyed quiet picnics alongside the upper reaches of the **Guiers Vif** – near its source. Our children have been content to spend their time, as long as we would allow them, paddling in the safe stream – building imaginary dams with the clean, rounded rocks that abound in mountain torrents. In October my eyes have feasted on the autumn shades of the dying leaves – a veritable palette of glorious golds, coppers, reds and browns; Walt Disney could hardly have bettered the colour-scapes on the steep hillsides.

The dense forests and green pastures of the high Chartreuse Massif reward those who give it three or four days of their time – you'll glow with the peaceful satisfaction that only Mother Nature seems to give; what better tonic could there be? To get the best out of the whole area use both Michelin yellow maps – 74 and 77. Head your car up as many of the *dead-end* roads as possible; you'll find that advice repeated throughout the pages of this small book – I'll give you some examples of what I mean in the Chartreuse Massif.

At the summit of the Col de Porte, bear west and then north up the lane that climbs steeply towards the **Charmant Som** peak. You'll have marvellous views and the dark, silent, dense forests to yourself. Explore the sources of the two strangely-named streams called the Guiers Vif and **Guiers Mort**: the first lies south-east of **St-Pierre-d'Entremont**; the second is to the south-east of **St-Pierre-de-Chartreuse**. Later drive through the narrow gorges of both streams as they descend steeply to the west.

A fourth and final example is the forest roads that lie to the south of the D520B linking **St-Laurent-du-Pont** and St-Pierre-de-Chartreuse. They require great care –

La Correrie just south of the Couvent de la Grande Chartreuse

but you'll enjoy every single moment of your exploration. The road that climbs to the **Col de la Charmette** and descends into the **Ténaison** Valley is particularly recommended. Once again you'll have these forest tracks to yourself.

The Gorges du Guiers Mort are to the immediate south of the world famous **Couvent de la Grande Chartreuse** – a monastery lost in a wooded fold of mountains. It's not possible to visit the buildings, founded in 1035 by Saint Bruno of the Carthusian Order; they have been destroyed and rebuilt many times during the centuries. You can however visit La Correrie – a museum set in a handsome building, showing the way of life of the Carthusian monks.

It was in La Grande Chartreuse that the Age of Steel was said to have been born in Europe during the 12th century; ancient records of the Carthusians have revealed this amazing truth.

Due west, and outside the mountain walls of the Massif, is the small town of **Voiron**. It's here that the legendary Chartreuse liqueurs are distilled. It is claimed that over 130 herbs from the mountain pastures are blended together at the distillery; three monks share a different part of the secret recipe, which was perfected as recently as 1764. Both the yellow and green liquids pack quite a punch; no wonder, as the lime-green variety – such a dry, elegant liqueur – is 96.3 per cent proof! Make certain you try them during your holiday.

Far to the east, under the eastern wall of the Chartreuse Massif, and at the foot of the Col du Granier, lie many of the vineyards of Savoie. You'll see the village names on many local wine lists: **Apremont** and **Abymes** (**Abîmes** on the map) are fresh, light whites; **Chignin** and **Montmélian** are reds – made from the Mondeuse grape.

50

You'll often see wines called by this grape type name.

Just north of Apremont is **Les Charmettes**, the house where Jean-Jacques Rousseau and Madame de Warens lived together from 1736 to 1742; much of his work must have been inspired by the rural life he enjoyed there, surrounded by its pastoral pleasures. The house is open to visitors.

Other attractions – away from villages and towns – will interest both adults and children alike. Two small lakes are set beyond the western borders of the Chartreuse: the **Lac d'Aiguebelette** and **Lac de Paladru**. Both have bathing facilities and also offer fishing and boating opportunities. Between the two lakes is **Les Echelles**; to the north-east of the village are caves called the **Grottes des Echelles** – the starting point for visits is on the N6.

Beyond the River Isère, on the eastern side of the Massif, is the Chemin de Fer Touristique du Bréda; a short, privately-owned railway running from **Pontcharra**, through the **Gorges du Bréda**, to **La Rochette**. Steam trains run from June to September; enquire locally for days and times of operation.

Further down the Isère Valley, 14 kilometres before you reach Grenoble, is the village of **Lancey**. It was here, in 1869, that Aristide Bergès first used *white coal* – captured water falling at great speed down steeply inclined pipes – in a practical way to turn the turbines of his paper-pulp mills.

For those of you who enjoy mountain-top views but prefer to reach them by mechanical means, two *téléphérique* trips are strongly recommended. The smaller and less spectacular one climbs up to the 1782 metres summit of **La Scia**, east of St-Pierre-de-Chartreuse. The second lies outside the Massif and to the south-east of

The Guiers Mort Valley: heading east into the glorious Chartreuse

Grenoble; it starts its huge lift up the 2257 metres high **Croix de Chamrousse** from the village of **Chamrousse** – a village reached by fine roads that run up through magnificent forests. The view from the *téléphérique* terminus is an astonishing and extensive one.

Grenoble and Chambéry deserve some of your time. Grenoble is a fine, modern and bustling city: see the older sections, alongside the southern bank of the Isère; enjoy the parks; and take the cable-car climb up to the Fort de la Bastille, high above the city on the north bank of the Isère. Chambéry is a much older and smaller town, once the capital of the Dukes of Savoie. It has a central, pedestrian-only area, and has many fine arcades and lovely shops. Both the château and cathedral should be on your visiting list in Chambéry. The town is also one of the main centres of the French *vermouth* industry; usually white, dry wines *aromatised* by bitter substances – the red ones are white wine coloured with caramel!

The Chartreuse is surrounded by the Alpine pastures of Savoie and Dauphiné; consequently it is very much dairy country. Milk, cream and cheese predominate in the regional dishes you'll be offered at countryside restaurants. *Gratins* appear everywhere; the most famous is the *gratin Dauphinois*, a dish of sliced potatoes covered with cream, cheese and the slightest flavouring of garlic. *French Leave* describes the cheeses of the region and the many fish that are caught in the mountain lakes to the north of the Chartreuse. Please also study other chapters covering neighbouring areas for details of further regional specialities. Finally, you'll see many walnut trees on your travels; these feature in many regional cake specialities.

COL DE LA PLACETTE   du Col
Simple hotel

This *Logis de France* – comprising two buildings – lies at the summit of the road
between **Voreppe** and **St-Laurent-du-Pont**. Apart from the Chartreuse mountains
it is also well sited for you to enjoy the *Vercors* to the south on the far side of the
River **Isère**. Good walking and riding from the hotel. Menus include *morilles à la
crème, omelette aux morilles* and delicious *fromage blanc*.
fpm A–C *meals* NC *rooms* 28 A–C *closed* Rest only: 1 Jan–mid Feb. Fri.
post Col de la Placette. 38340 Voreppe. Isère. *phone* (76) 50.04.65.

COL DE PORTE   Chalet Hôtel Rogier
Simple hotel/Secluded

A modern chalet-style hotel, well maintained and in a superb site 1350 metres above
sea-level. You'll find it on the road from the Col de Porte to the summit of **Charmant
Som**, in magnificent wooded country. It is popular at weekends in the winter – when
the pastures near the hotel make ideal, easy terrain for skiing. There are fine views
and walks in every direction – it's all perfection
fpm A–C *meals* NC *rooms* 18 B–C *closed* 1 Nov–Xmas. Rest only: Tues (July–Sept).
post Col de Porte. 38700 La Tronche. Isère. *phone* (76) 08.82.04.

ST-PIERRE-DE-CHARTREUSE   Beau Site
Comfortable hotel/Swimming pool

An extremely smart modernised building in the higher part of St-Pierre-de-
Chartreuse, as you climb towards the **Col du Cucheron**. A tiny swimming pool has
been added to the hotel alongside the road – from it you get marvellous views to the
south. Enjoy the strangely-named torrent called the **Guiers Mort** and the cool
woods and pastures to the north.
fpm A–C *meals* NC *rooms* 34 B–D *closed* Mid Oct–mid Dec.
post St-Pierre. 38380 St-Laurent-du-Pont. Isère. *phone* (76) 08.61.34.

ST-PIERRE-DE-CHARTREUSE   Aub. Atre Fleuri
Simple restaurant with rooms/Quiet

A really simple place, on the D512 and a few kilometres to the south of St-Pierre-de-
Chartreuse. It's a pity though that caravans dot many of the pastures nearby to spoil,
just a bit, this isolated spot. However, those eyesores will not prevent you enjoying
many good dishes: *truites* (in various forms), *jambon cru de montagne* and *neige à
la liqueur de Chartreuse*.
fpm A–B *meals* C *rooms* 8 A–B *closed* 1 Nov–mid Dec. Tues evg and Wed (out of
season). *post* St-Pierre. 38380 St-Laurent-du-Pont. Isère. *phone* (76) 08.60.21.

CORRÈZE

9

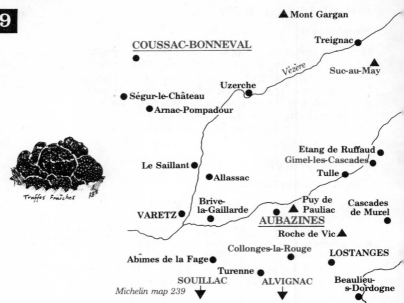

Mont Gargan ▲

COUSSAC-BONNEVAL
●

Treignac ●

Vézère

Suc-au-May ▲

Uzerche
●

● Ségur-le-Château
● Arnac-Pompadour

Truffes Fraîches

Etang de Ruffaud ●
Gimel-les-Cascades ●

Le Saillant ●

Tulle ●

● Allassac

Brive-
la-Gaillarde
●

Puy de
▲ Pauliac

Cascades
de Murel
●

VARETZ ●

AUBAZINES

Roche de Vic ▲

Collonges-la-Rouge
●

LOSTANGES
●

Abîmes de la Fage ●

Turenne ●

SOUILLAC ▼

ALVIGNAC ▼

Beaulieu-
s-Dordogne

Michelin map 239

For Anglo-Saxons there is no more popular area in France than the Dordogne. That descriptive term – as understood by visitors – isn't necessarily the *département* of Dordogne, or the mighty river that rises in the volcanic hills of Auvergne and flows generally westwards to eventually join forces with the Garonne; rather, it's the pocket of country that is adjacent to the south-west edges of my map. The vast majority of visitors to that tourist area called the Dordogne ignore my area, which I have named Corrèze; it's situated, more or less, within the boundaries of the *département* known by that name.

Corrèze is still particularly unspoilt and its tiny and numerous lanes are as inviting as ever, lost amongst the finest trees in France. Mother Nature works wonders in these hills: in May and June the endless varieties of trees are at their most beautiful, exploding into life with the vitality and freshness of all the new tints of green; in September and October the glorious autumn shades are at their best. In the higher hills to the east the pastures are an equal delight: in spring the meadows are full of the yellows and whites of wild flowers – narcissi, celandines, cowslips, wild daffodils, snowdrops and violets; in the autumn it is the turn of the lilac-shaded autumn crocus, tiny dianthus and spiraea. I implore you to discover Corrèze for yourself; the more you run the risk of getting lost here, the more certain you are of seeing *Hidden France*.

Let's start our look at this jewel box of France at the point the River **Dordogne** enters the *département* of Corrèze on the eastern boundary – in the neighbourhood of **Bort-les-Orgues**. Above the small town to the west are strange organ-like rock formations; but it is a man-made marvel that competes for the traveller's attention –

see page 60

ST-DEZERY ●
Ussel ●

Corrèze

Egletons ●
Château de Ventadour ●

Puy de
Manzagol

Château de Val

Site de
St-Nazaire

Bort-les-
Orgues

Neuvic

Rhue

Barrage de Marèges

édière

● Clergoux

Dordogne

Barrage de l'Aigle

MENTHE

ST-PARDOUX-LA-CROISILLE

Barrage du Chastang

Maronne

Servières-le-Château

Tours de Merle

see page 30

Argentat

SOUSCEYRAC

the mighty Barrage de Bort. It holds back a 15 kilometres long narrow lake – and it is the first of many massive hydro-electric dams that make the Dordogne such a rewarding river for this part of France. The **Château de Val**, on the eastern bank, is perhaps one of the most photographed in France; you will undoubtedly have seen it on many a tourist brochure or poster. The lake offers bathing, boating and a variety of water sports. Before you leave the general area of Bort, explore the splendid gorges of the **Rhue** Valley to the east of the town.

We will return to the northern parts of Corrèze later, but for the moment let's continue downstream on the Dordogne, making the occasional sortie up into the hills that lie on both sides of the river. First, desert the river at Bort and head west to the **Site de St-Nazaire** – a vast panorama unfolds below you. You will see the second of the lakes formed by another dam, but to spot the structure itself you must use the roads to the west of the lake and detour to the **Barrage de Marèges**. Man has reduced the Dordogne into an impotent river these days; 100 years ago it must have been a superb sight.

Double back to the lake that lies in the green, wooded hills to the east of **Neuvic**. If you drive the narrow lanes that circle it you'll get a series of pretty views of the placid waters; climb the **Puy de Manzagol** and you'll win a panoramic vista of the whole man-made stretch of water. Further west still from the lake are the ruins of the once impregnable fortress called the **Château de Ventadour**. Nearby **Egletons** is in the countryside where – in Frederick Forsyth's *The Day of the Jackal* – the Jackal murdered Colette!

Don't use the road that goes due south from Neuvic, but rather the D168 which is described as the Route des Ajustants, which shows another part of the river off to great advantage – the long, winding strip of water that is held back by the mighty **Barrage de l'Aigle**. Don't bypass it – it's an amazing sight.

Cross to the northern banks of the Dordogne once again and head for **Clergoux**. You'll see for yourself the woods of Corrèze which I admire so much; seek out the Renaissance château at Sédière, just to the north-west of Clergoux. It's a perfect example of what I am continually urging you to do – use *dead-end* lanes as often as time permits. Your reward here will be the warming thrill one gets on discovering an exquisite corner of countryside; small lakes, superb trees and a handsome man-made structure combine to perfection.

The last of the Dordogne dams I ask you to look at is one of the largest – certainly its power station produces more electricity than any of the others – the **Barrage du Chastang**. Detour a few kilometres south-east to view the village of **Servières-le-Château**, perched above the River Glane. If you have time – what a wretched enemy that is – continue due south to another river valley, the **Maronne**. Matching the splendour of the scenic treasures is a man-made special – the ruins of the 900 year old fortress, identified on the map as **Tours de Merle** and impregnable in its day; a really spectacular *son et lumière* spectacle takes place here every evening during the high season.

After this scenic detour make **Argentat** your next port of call, where man and Nature have combined their talents to put on a thoroughly satisfying *show*; the small town, on the banks of the Dordogne, has a perfect river setting, seen at its best from the bridge. South of the town the river at last begins to resemble the one

The château at Sédière: a perfect example of *hidden* France

known by the hundreds of thousands of visitors who see it only in its lower stretches. Follow the western bank to **Beaulieu-s-Dordogne**, long famous for its Romanesque Eglise St-Pierre, built by monks from Cluny in the 12th century; its special treasure is a tympanum of the Last Supper over the south door.

A series of attractions lie downstream – off my map and heading into tourist-frequented country; but I suggest you ignore them and instead head back into those superb hills. Find **Collonges-la-Rouge**; it is a unique place, where the houses and the church are built of red sandstone. It will take you back hundreds of years – you will linger there longer than time allows, I promise you. You can then head west via **Turenne**, an old village dominated by the ruins of a great castle, to the **Abîmes de la Fage**. Nature reminds you here that she, too, can capture your attention and weave her own spell; underground caves full of fascinating stalagmites and stalactites.

Alternatively, at Collonges-la-Rouge you could head north-east, using the narrow, tree-lined lanes that ascend, higher and higher, eventually reaching the peak called **Roche de Vic**. It's a marvellous viewpoint with a panorama that is a *sea* of trees in all directions. If the weather has been wet, or if it is early spring, seek out, a little way to the north-east, the *dead-end* track that takes you to the **Cascades de Murel**, *lost* in the dense forests.

From either of these two beauty spots head north-west to another splendid viewpoint – the summit of the **Puy de Pauliac**. Below you is the small, attractive village of **Aubazines** – don't miss its ancient, 12th century Cistercian abbey. Descend to the **Corrèze** Valley; downstream lies busy **Brive-la-Gaillarde** – but my preference is to take you in the opposite direction, upstream.

Beyond **Tulle**, on the River Montane (it flows into the Corrèze), is tiny **Gimel-les-Cascades**; you will gasp at the sight of the three superb waterfalls in this exciting bit of river country. I've had the thrill of seeing it at its best in early spring – a real extrovert show; do see it. Seek out the **Etang de Ruffaud**, a small lake set amidst woods of pine, oak and birch.

What of the northern stretches of the *département* of Corrèze? You may have entered it heading south on the N20 from Limoges. To the west of that busy highway are three places you should seek out: tiny **Coussac-Bonneval** with a château and its splendid pointed towers; the super riverside setting of equally tiny **Ségur-le-Château**, dominated by the ruins of its 12th century castle; and finally the town of **Arnac-Pompadour** – in 1745 Louis XV gave the château here and the title of Marchionness to the renowned Madame de Pompadour. It's more famous these days for its magnificent National Stud; you can visit the stables. The small town also has one of the most attractive *hippodromes* (racecourses) I've seen.

To the east of the N20 are three worthy detours: the 731 metres summit of **Mont Gargan** with its vast panorama; the even higher **Suc-au-May** viewpoint with its own immense views – the surrounding hills are renowned for their heather and bilberries; and between them the attractive town of **Treignac**, alongside the **Vézère**. That stream offers an unusual way of enjoying the last of these northern corners of Corrèze; follow the river downstream to **Uzerche**, which is on the N20 – it's a splendid place, encircled by a loop of the river. Continue on downstream, seeking out the views from the bridge at **Le Saillant** and the ancient town of **Allassac**.

58   An ideal picnic spot near Sédière

AUBAZINES   de la Tour
Simple hotel/Quiet

The village is situated high above the **Corrèze** Valley; opposite the hotel is the splendid façade of the 12th century Cistercian abbey. It's a smart *Logis de France* and, in the opinion of Michelin, offers particularly good-value meals. But there was nothing regional about the cuisine when I was there; *avocat mayonnaise* and *œufs à la neige* were two of the dishes on the menu.

fpm A–B *meals* NC *rooms* 20 A–B *closed* Jan. Fri evg (Oct–May).
post Aubazines. 19190 Beynat. Corrèze. *phone* (55) 25.71.17.

COUSSAC-BONNEVAL   Voyageurs
Comfortable restaurant with rooms/Quiet/GC

A vine-covered place sitting in the shadow of the château. Be certain to visit nearby **Arnac-Pompadour** – the horse centre of France. The Roberts are renowned for their high standard of cuisine; you'll enjoy *confit de canard, terrine du chef, salade Limousine, caille rôtie, crépinette de ris de veau au foie gras* and the *cèpes* that appear in many dishes.

fpm A–B *meals* NC *rooms* 12 A–C *closed* Jan. Feb. Mon (Oct–Mar).
post Coussac-Bonneval. 87500 St-Yriex-la-Perche. H.-Vienne. *phone* (55) 75.20.24.

ST-DEZERY   Les Gravades
Comfortable hotel/Quiet

Corrèze is called *Le Pays Vert* – and how true that is; there seems to be timber everywhere. This modern, futuristic-looking building is on the N89, four kilometres north-east of **Ussel**; it also makes a good base for the area I've called *Creuse*. Good basic cuisine with dishes like *confit de canard, gigot d'agneau aux herbes* and *filet de truite à l'oseille*.

fpm A–C *meals* C *rooms* 17 C–D *closed* Rest only: Fri evg & Sat midday (out of season).
post St-Dezery. 19200 Ussel. Corrèze. *phone* (55) 72.21.53.

ST-PARDOUX-LA-CROISILLE   Beau Site
Comfortable hotel/Quiet/Terrace/Gardens/Swimming pool/Tennis

What utter perfection at this isolated hotel hidden in the forests to the north of the River **Dordogne**. It has everything: apart from the list of attractions above it has terraces which face south, a lovely view of the pinewoods to the rear and an ever-increasing reputation for excellent cuisine. Both local dishes and lighter *nouvelle cuisine* specialities appear on the menus.

fpm A–D *meals* C *rooms* 35 C–D *closed* Oct–Apl. *phone* (55) 27.85.44.
post St-Pardoux-la-Croisille. 19320 Marcillac-la-Croisille. Corrèze.

CREUSE

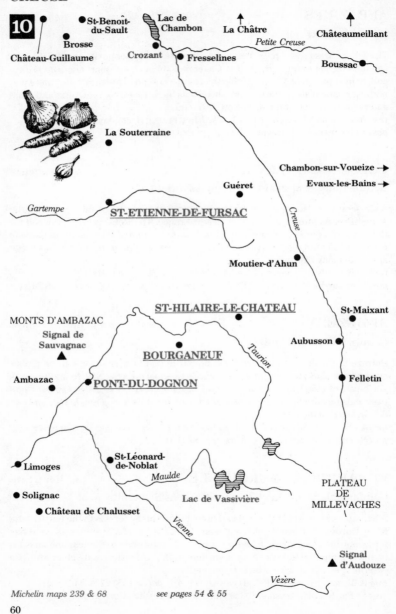

10

Château-Guillaume

● St-Benoît-du-Sault

● Brosse

Lac de Chambon

La Châtre ↑

Châteaumeillant ↑

Petite Creuse

Crozant ● Fresselines

Boussac ●

La Souterraine ●

Chambon-sur-Voueize →

Evaux-les-Bains →

Guéret ●

Gartempe

ST-ETIENNE-DE-FURSAC

Creuse

Moutier-d'Ahun ●

ST-HILAIRE-LE-CHATEAU ●

St-Maixant ●

MONTS D'AMBAZAC

Signal de Sauvagnac ▲

Taurion

Aubusson ●

BOURGANEUF ●

Ambazac ●

PONT-DU-DOGNON ●

Felletin ●

Limoges ●

St-Léonard-de-Noblat ●

Maulde

Solignac ●

Lac de Vassivière

PLATEAU DE MILLEVACHES

Château de Chalusset ●

Vienne

Signal d'Audouze ▲

Vézère

This area, more than any other, is probably known by no more than one per cent of my readers. The *départements* of Creuse (most of it is the area enclosed within the boundaries of my map); Corrèze (the subject of the previous chapter); and Haute-Vienne (some of it is on the left side of my map, but much of it is to the west of Limoges) make up the region called Limousin. That whole region can hardly be called one of the more popular holiday areas of France. Creuse most certainly is a part of Limousin where the visitor will win benefits of a less obvious kind: utter peace and quiet; for the most part gentler scenic aspects; and hotels and restaurants (though there are not many of them) where good value counts more than exceptional abilities in cuisine.

In my book *French Leave* I wrote that Limousin – together with the Auvergne – is a gastronomic desert when compared with other parts of France. However, don't be put off by this – the area compensates in many other ways. There are not many regional specialities to look for – but amongst them are: *farcidure* – a dumpling, either poached or sautéed; *mique* – a stew of dumplings; and, best of all, *clafoutis* – pancake batter, poured over fruit (usually black cherries in Limousin) and then baked. The delicious *cèpes* of Limousin – fine, delicate, flap mushrooms – are another, not to be missed, treat. The region gives its name to a famous reddish-coloured breed of cattle – like the white-coated Charolais variety they give a high yield of quality meat. You may see on wine lists **Châteaumeillant** wines; these are made from Gamay grapes (the Beaujolais grape type) and come from a small area near that town, just off the northern edges of my map.

The last named town, or nearby **La Châtre** – associated with, and beloved by, George Sand – would make a good gateway to the north-east corner of Creuse. Alternatively, you may have feasted on the many ancient, man-made pleasures hidden in the river valleys east of Poitiers: St-Savin, Fontgombault and Mont-morillon are examples; and this would bring you into the north-western corner of my map. Whichever direction you approach from, make the **Creuse** Valley your first objective. River valleys are going to play an important part in my description – and your exploration – of this area. Four major French rivers rise in the **Plateau de Millevaches** – the area in the bottom right-hand corner of my map: the Creuse itself, the Cher, the **Vienne** and the **Vézère** (see the chapter called *Corrèze*). I'll describe that strangely-named and unusual area in more detail later on.

The north-east approach is particularly magnificent in late May or early June when the gentle hills glow far brighter than the sun itself. Golden broom is the reason; you'll not see more brilliant colours anywhere else in France. Your route should eventually head for **Guéret** – but first make a deviation to the man-made **Lac de Chambon**. The Barrage d'Eguzon is the cause of this long lake being formed by the waters of the Creuse. Well before the dam was built, in 1926, the valley was adored by both painters and writers; and made famous by George Sand, Théodore Rousseau and Claude Monet. All the stretch from Argenton, just north of my map, upstream to **Fresselines** is lovely country. At **Crozant** are the ruins of what was once a powerful fortress. In the Middle Ages its great walls and ramparts – one kilometre long – played an important part in both the Hundred Years War and the Wars of Religion.

If you have approached from the north-west, your objectives should be the same

A rare sight now in modern France: near Lac de Vassivière

as described in the previous paragraph but, on your way to the Creuse Valley, seek out lost **Château-Guillaume**, a tiny village in the Allemette Valley dwarfed by its castle; and the equally lost ruins of the castle at **Brosse**. Both these splendours are to the west of ancient **St-Benoît-du-Sault**.

Both approaches will now allow you to enjoy the kindly, quiet pleasures of the Creuse Valley. From Fresselines you can head south to Guéret – a busy market town with a super local museum which houses handsome exhibits of medieval Limousin enamels, a collection of dolls and Aubusson tapestries. Another treasure in the town is the nearby Hôtel des Moneyroux, similar to the Palais Jacques-Cœur in Bourges, to the north-east of Creuse.

Alternatively, from Fresselines, you could head east, enjoying the countryside straddling the small tributary of the Creuse called the **Petite Creuse**. **Boussac** is dominated by its medieval castle – associated, like so much of this area, with George Sand and a character by the name of Prince Zizim – more about him later. South-east of Boussac is a delightful pocket of country adjacent to the upper reaches of the Cher: **Chambon-sur-Voueize** has its 900 year old Eglise Ste-Valérie; nearby **Evaux-les-Bains** was valued by the Romans for its curative spa waters. After this simple *deviation* return west to Guéret.

From Guéret I suggest you make a great clockwise sweep that will eventually take you to a point east of **Limoges**. I ask you to make great use of your Michelin map again as, the more obscure the roads you use are, the more you'll enjoy the pastoral scenic vistas that abound in the green landscape. All the lovely wooded country south of Guéret is interlaced with a huge number of lanes; head up them and see at first-hand what I mean. The first man-made highlight you should seek out is the abbey church at **Moutier-d'Ahun,** near the Creuse; its famous woodwork, carved 300 years ago, is superb.

The next port of call up the Creuse Valley should be **Aubusson** – world famous for its celebrated tapestries and carpets. Both this town and its nearby neighbour, **Felletin**, flourished centuries ago; tapestry making fell into decline in the 19th century but during the last 40 years Jean Lurcat has restored its fame with a modern approach to the skilled art. Exhibitions of the tapestry makers' skills can be visited at both centres. Spare time also for the castle at **St-Maixant** (just north-east of Aubusson) – its towers and moat are worth the detour.

Head south into the strangely-named Plateau de Millevaches – a tableland of countless springs. Its name does not originate from *vaches* (cows) but from the old Celtic word *batz* – meaning spring. It is lonely, wild country – full of granite rocks and pine forests. The best panoramas are from the **Signal d'Audouze**; you'll have to make a short climb on Shanks's pony from the D36 to reach this 953 metres high viewpoint, close to the point where the Vienne springs into life.

North-west now to the man-made **Lac de Vassivière**. You can drive around the many inlets of this little-known lake; and yet there is every kind of water sport available – bathing, boating, canoeing, yachting, motor-boats and the chance for a *pédalo* ride. The fisherman, too, is well looked after. It's the River **Maulde** that has formed this large, unusually shaped, artificial lake; the river is a tributary of the Vienne and in its very short life it really does work for its living. Starting with the dam at the lake, there are no less than eight dams as you follow the lanes along its banks downstream to **St-Léonard-de-Noblat** (there is a signposted route); this old town is well worth exploring – particularly splendid is the belfry of the 11th century church.

Before doing that river trip you could make a short dash north to **Bourganeuf** – its medieval tower was the prison for Prince Zizim, a Mohammedan prince who took refuge in the town in 1483. All this terrain is attractive country – beech trees now appear with pines; it's decidedly more pleasant than the Millevaches Plateau.

All that remains for you to explore now is a ring of country to the east of Limoges and the fine, busy town itself. **La Souterraine** is a centuries-old town with an 800 year old church and examples of its original fortifications still stand, in the form of the Porte St-Jean and the Porte Notre-Dame. Between the town and Limoges are pleasant hills called the **Monts d'Ambazac**; its highest point is the **Signal de Sauvagnac** – you can see the Puy de Dôme far to the east. **Ambazac** itself is famous for its magnificent *treasure*.

To the immediate south of Limoges are two man-made sights: the 12th century abbey church in the village of **Solignac**; and the ruins of another 12th century masterpiece – this one a formidable fortress called the **Château de Chalusset**.

Limoges is world famous for its centuries-old tradition of making decorative enamels and its equally renowned porcelain work. Many workshops can be visited to see just how the enamels are produced; the Municipal Museum houses a huge display of them – covering the centuries. The Musée National Adrien Dubouché has some 10,000 examples of porcelain work. The old town, a cathedral and several churches are all additional highlights.

The ruins of the château at Chalusset, south of Limoges

BOURGANEUF
Moulin de Montaletang

Comfortable hotel/Secluded/Terrace/Gardens/GC

What a gorgeous place; a restored and extended mill, alongside a stream, lost in the forests 13 kilometres south of the town (follow the signs from the Limoges road). Apart from the streams, *étangs* and lovely trees, there is the bonus of really good cooking with emphasis given to the lighter style of today: *chausson de langoustines au bisque* and *fricassée de volailles au vinaigre du cidre* are examples.

fpm A–C *meals* NC *rooms* 14 B–D *closed* Dec–Easter. Wed evg & Thurs midday (out of season). *post* 23400 Bourganeuf. Creuse. *phone* (55) 64.92.72.

PONT-DU-DOGNON
Rallye

Comfortable hotel/Secluded/Terrace

An extremely smart-looking modern place, facing south and overlooking the **Taurion** Valley – at this point a flooded, narrow lake. For many years the hotel has been known for its good-value menus. There's nothing exceptional about them but good use is made of many Limousin products: *truites*, *omelette aux cèpes* and *jambon de campagne* illustrate this well.

fpm A–B *meals* NC *rooms* 20 B–D *closed* Mid Nov–end Jan. (Book out of season.) *post* Pont-du-Dognon. 87340 Jonchères-St-Maurice. H.-Vienne. *phone* (55) 56.56.11.

ST-ETIENNE-DE-FURSAC
Moderne

Simple hotel/Gardens

Another modern, smart-looking building – opposite the church and within 50 metres of the infant River **Gartempe**; later in its life that stream flows past the truly magnificent Romanesque church at St-Savin (100 kilometres to the north). *Pâté de canard* and *magret de canard* are amongst the specialities; others include *cèpes* and *écrevisses*; and for dessert – *crêpes soufflées au Cointreau*.

fpm A–D *meals* C *rooms* 14 A–D *closed* Mid–end Oct. Mid–end Feb. Sun evg & Mon midday (out of season). *post* 23290 St-Etienne-de-Fursac. Creuse. *phone* (55) 63.60.56.

ST-HILAIRE-LE-CHATEAU
du Thaurion

Comfortable hotel/Terrace/GC

A modernised *Logis de France* with ambitious owners who have already made an impression with their mixture of regional dishes and *nouvelle cuisine*. Amongst the former are *La Brejaude (soupe aux choux)* and *clafoutis*; amongst the many newer dishes are *lotte au St-Emilion et au concombre* and *cuisse de poulette à la vapeur de truffes et de girolles*. There's delightful country to the south.

fpm A–D *meals* NC *rooms* 10 D–E *closed* Dec–Feb. Wed (mid Sept–June). *post* St-Hilaire-le-Château. 23250 Pontarion. Creuse. *phone* (55) 64.50.12.

LES DOMBES

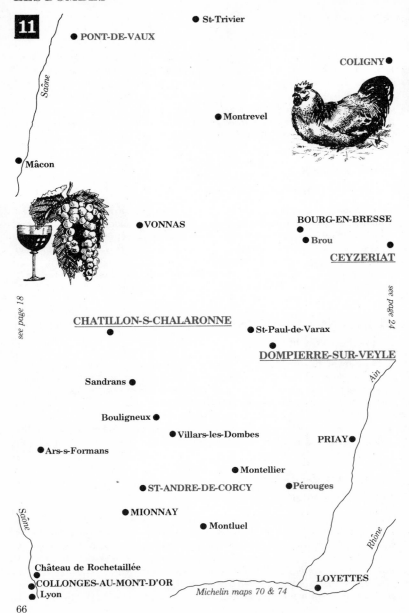

11

● St-Trivier

● PONT-DE-VAUX

COLIGNY●

Saône

● Montrevel

● Mâcon

BOURG-EN-BRESSE

●VONNAS

● Brou

CEYZERIAT

see page 18

see page 24

CHATILLON-S-CHALARONNE

● St-Paul-de-Varax

DOMPIERRE-SUR-VEYLE

Ain

Sandrans ●

Bouligneux ●

●Villars-les-Dombes

PRIAY●

●Ars-s-Formans

● Montellier

● **ST-ANDRE-DE-CORCY**

●Pérouges

● **MIONNAY**

Saône

● Montluel

Rhône

Château de Rochetaillée

COLLONGES-AU-MONT-D'OR

LOYETTES

● Lyon

Michelin maps 70 & 74

What a strange landscape – but alluring, too, in its own special way – is the countryside of Les Dombes. Yet, 99 per cent of all the endless tourists, speeding down the autoroutes and highways that line its western borders, choose to ignore its unique and very captivating charms.

What are those particular delights? Les Dombes (part of the Bresse countryside) is a huge peppered-landscape of *étangs* – the French word for ponds or pools. Two thousand or so of them, of all sizes, dot the emerald-green, flat countryside that lies within the triangle of **Mâcon**, **Bourg-en-Bresse** and **Lyon**. The *étangs* and the marsh-like fields that surround them are full of wildlife. My family and I have idled away many inquisitive hours – full of quiet pleasure – on the edges of some of those pools, watching the comings and goings of the endless varieties of birds. Arm yourself with a pair of binoculars and do the same. At **Villars-les-Dombes** there is an excellent bird sanctuary. In this reserve, set out as a park, are many hundreds of different species; some come and go on the many pools, others are to be found in large, *open* cages. Don't, under any circumstances, miss it.

A picnic lunch underneath a shady tree is the perfect way to go bird watching. Equally, my family has enjoyed picnic lunches – and breakfasts – alongside the banks of the River **Ain**, which is ideal for paddling and shady slumber. How many of you with young families – on motoring holidays – can remember those frequent occasions when, around about midday, you begin to look for suitable picnic spots? Once you start the search, mile after mile passes without a suitable spot appearing: not enough shade; too much shade; too close to the road; too many ants; too much of this; not enough of that. The only answer is to turn left or right up a minor road and soon you'll find a suitable spot where all members of the family will be happy enough. In Les Dombes, up the minor roads, you'll find plenty of ideal places that are close enough to the meres and pools.

Then use all the myriad lanes that abound in every direction to discover other hidden pleasures. A handful of interesting old châteaux and churches are to be found at **Bouligneux**, **Sandrans**, **Ars-s-Formans**, **Montellier**, **St-Paul-de-Varax** and at Villars itself. Search out the attractive village of **Châtillon-s-Chalaronne**; it has changed out of all recognition over a period of 20 years – now spotless and a mass of flowers (one of many *villages fleuris* in the area). The ancient covered market place, the old houses and the River Chalaronne are special highlights; you'll linger long in this attractive, seductive place.

To the north of Châtillon is another *village fleuri* – **Vonnas**. This small place has become world famous because of the Blanc family who are legends in Bresse country. La Mère Blanc – a famous Bressan *cuisinière* – started it all; now her grandson, Georges Blanc, not yet 40, continues the tradition – he recently won the coveted third Michelin star. Another three star chef in Les Dombes is Alain Chapel, who, in less than two decades, has transformed his father's restaurant, Chez la Mère Charles, into one of the world's great restaurants. Dozens of fine restaurants are to be found in Bresse country; no other small area in the world has such a formidable and fantastic concentration of cuisine skill.

All the ingredients these many talented chefs need to ply their trade so skilfully are close at hand: wines from **Beaujolais** and **Bugey**; cheeses from their own *pays* and also from the hills of Jura and Savoie; fresh vegetables from Provence; beef

Pérouges: the heart of this perfect small fortified town

from the magnificent Charolais cattle of southern Burgundy; *écrevisses* (crayfish) and trout from the streams; and superb fish from the River **Saône** and the lakes to the east in the Savoie mountains. Bresse itself is famous for its *grenouilles* (frogs) and especially for its incomparable chickens.

The world-famous reputation of these Bressan chickens has been developed and perfected over many centuries. The fattened fowl, with the most white and tender flesh, are equally enjoyable whether served with a rich cream sauce, in some *nouvelle cuisine* creation or as a simple *poularde de Bresse rôtie*.

Several other sights deserve your attention; try not to miss any of them. The first is in the south-east corner of the area, at **Pérouges**. It is a remarkable hilltop citadel. Four centuries ago it was a busy, thriving place; three centuries later it had all but fallen into ruin. Its original population of some 2,000 souls had dwindled to no more than 50 or so; main roads were rebuilt away from it and the new railways passed it by. At the turn of this century it was even threatened with demolition. Thankfully, many local people fought that outrageous suggestion and started a campaign to have the place restored. Today, as you walk the narrow streets, soaking up the dream-like atmosphere that shrouds its ancient stone houses, give thanks to the far-sighted individuals who fought so hard to preserve Pérouges. Seek out the lime tree in its centre that was planted 200 years ago. By all means enjoy the fortified fortress during daylight – no cars are allowed to spoil the pleasure of walking the narrow, cobbled streets; but, take my advice, come back in the twilight and see it at its best.

Throughout France are many hundreds of small roadside monuments — placed there to the memory of local heroes of the Resistance. One typical example of this is an obscure memorial at the side of the road that leads down from Pérouges to the N84; you'll find it just 200 metres or so before the main road – lost in the hedge, where two patriots were shot by the Germans on 1st September 1944. It is yet another poignant reminder of how many sickening murders were carried out in the name of *War* during those bitter occupation years of the Second World War.

35 kilometres to the north is Bourg-en-Bresse; a largish town which will not disappoint you if you walk its old and new streets. But its main treasure lies to the south of the town at **Brou**. Put an hour or two aside to enjoy the Eglise de Brou, a magnificent Gothic building full of interest. My wife and I have quietly walked within its ancient walls and cool cloisters on many occasions; and have enjoyed the many fascinating exhibits in the adjoining monastery which now houses the Ain Museum – showing aspects of the Bressan way of life during the centuries. North of Bourg are many super examples of restored Bressan farmhouses; seek out the Ferme de la Forêt at **St-Trivier** and the Ferme du Sougey at **Montrevel**. Their Sarrasine chimneys are particularly interesting.

Lyon – a vibrant, thriving city if ever there was one – is on the southern border of Les Dombes. The purpose of this book is not to pinpoint the attractions of the large cities and towns, but to encourage you to seek out the seductive pleasures of the countryside. The next suggestion however is part of the Lyon suburbs but it is easy to find and get to, being well clear of the city: the **Château de Rochetaillée** is to the north of Lyon, alongside the eastern bank of the River Saône, and it houses the Musée de l'Automobile Henri Malartre. Some of the most celebrated and earliest makes of car are amongst the 200 or so exhibits – some being quite unique; other exhibits include many famous racing cars from past decades. Unless you are totally allergic to such things I implore you not to miss this fine museum — attractively floodlit at night.

Another spectacle of the man-made kind is the final section of the astonishing new railway line that has been built from Paris to Lyon and opened in late 1981. The line goes due north from Lyon and skirts the western edges of Les Dombes before it crosses the River Saône, just south of Mâcon (where a new station has been built). If you can use the TGV trains (*Trains à Grande Vitesse* – very high speed) of the future, so much the better – they operate at 260/300 kilometres per hour (160/190 miles per hour); it could be just a short hop from Mâcon to Lyon. But, even if you can't do that, make certain you watch the trains as they speed along the specially built track; you'll have many opportunities to do that in the flat marshland to the immediate west of Châtillon-sur-Chalaronne. Notice how carefully the track has been planned. Because of shock waves as two trains pass each other, the twin tracks are some 5 metres apart and sharp curves have been completely avoided, only one curve having a tighter radius than four kilometres. Track gradients are far steeper than the normal lines in France.

Michelin map 74 is an absolute must if you are to get the best from this unusual countryside. It is a strange sight indeed when you examine the area on that map, but your efforts in navigating the lanes themselves – doing the real thing – will be greatly rewarded, I assure you. *French Leave* offers you many additional recommendations where you can eat and sleep so well in this, the greatest of all the culinary larders to be found on the face of the earth.

Ferme de la Forêt at St-Trivier with its unusual Sarrasine chimney

CEYZERIAT   Mont-July
Simple hotel/Quiet/Terrace/Gardens

A charming *Logis de France* eight kilometres to the east of that lovely town **Bourg-en-Bresse**. On a clear day there's a vast view across Les Dombes to the *Beaujolais* hills on the west bank of the River **Saône**. The hotel is ideally placed for the *Jura* and *Bugey*, too. Enjoy dishes like *grenouilles Mont-July, foie gras en brioche, caille, fromage blanc à la crème* and *fraises Melba*.
fpm A–C *meals* C *rooms* 19 A–C *closed* Mid Oct–mid Mar. Thurs (mid Mar–mid June). *post* 01250 Ceyzériat. Ain. *phone* (74) 30.00.12.

CHATILLON-SUR-CHALARONNE   Chevalier–Norbet
Comfortable hotel

Much the smarter and bigger of the two entries for this fascinating small town – one of the best of the many *villages fleuris* in Ain. Enjoy the river and also the fine covered market place which is hundreds of years old. Ambitious menus list specialities such as *poisson de mer, œufs brouillés aux morilles et aux truffes* and *poularde de Bresse à la crème*. See the triptych at the nearby Hôtel de Ville.
fpm B–D *meals* C *rooms* 29 B–E *closed* Jan. Rest only: Mon.
post Av. C. Desormes. 01400 Châtillon-s-Chalaronne. Ain. *phone* (74) 55.02.22.

CHATILLON-SUR-CHALARONNE   de la Tour
Comfortable restaurant with rooms

A much simpler place than the Chevalier-Norbet – this one is a *Logis de France*. I liked the great attention to detail: for example, the professionally printed menu. This took great advantage of the fine Bresse raw materials — witness some of the offerings: *pâté chaud de volaille, terrine de Bressane, caille des Dombes, grenouilles meunière* and *quenelle de brochet*.
fpm A–C *meals* C *rooms* 12 A–D *closed* Mid Feb–mid Mar. Wed. Sun evg (out of season). *post* Pl. République. 01400 Châtillon-s-Chalaronne. *phone* (74) 55.05.12.

DOMPIERRE-SUR-VEYLE   Aubert
Very simple rest. with rooms (no showers or baths)

Probably the simplest, most humble entry in *Hidden France* with a well-earned reputation locally for good cooking. If you prefer, use the *French Leave* base (*sans restaurant*) at **St-André-de-Corcy**, or a new find – Le Petit Casset at **Montluel** (postcode 01120); it's quiet and has a pool. Dishes here include *truite, grenouilles, poulet à la crème, vacherin praliné* and *omelette Norvégienne*.
fpm A–B *meals* NC *rooms* 3 A *closed* Feb. Mon evg. Thurs evg. Fri.
post Dompierre-sur-Veyle. 01240 St-Paul-de-Varax. Ain. *phone* (74) 30.31.19.

DOUBS

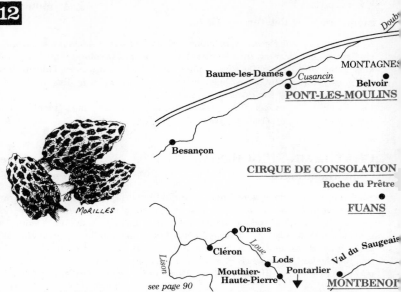

12

MORILLES

MONTAGNE
Baume-les-Dames ● *Cusancin*
Belvoir ●
PONT-LES-MOULINS

● Besançon

CIRQUE DE CONSOLATION
Roche du Prêtre ●
FUANS

● Ornans
● Cléron
Lods ●
Mouthier-
Haute-Pierre
see page 90
Pontarlier
Val du Saugeais
MONTBENOÎT

This chapter takes a look at the northern extremities of the Jura range of hills; the area it covers corresponds more or less to the *département* of Doubs, but the principal reason why I have given it this name – Doubs – is because of the splendid river that loops, in a huge circle, around this piece of lovely countryside. I encourage you to cross the river to the east, into the same Jura hills that lie in Switzerland. Another part of the Jura hills, to the south, is discussed in the chapter called *Jura*.

I have divided this chapter into basically three parts – each of them looking, in turn, at three river valleys, all so different in character and size: the **Doubs** itself; the tiny **Dessoubre**; and the **Loue**

The journey begins just north of **Pontarlier** at a point where the River Doubs has flowed north for about 40 kilometres from its source – at **Montbenoît**. This minute place sits alongside the Doubs in the **Val du Saugeais**; its special claim to fame is its ancient abbey, full of treasures.

The Val du Saugeais continues north-east along the Doubs until you reach **Morteau**, a very much bigger, modern place and known for its watchmaking; it was devastated by a fire over a century ago. The town gives its name to a famous fat sausage called *Jésus de Morteau*, which is smoked over pine and juniper. Another speciality of this particular valley is *brési* – wafer-thin slices of dried beef, similar to the well-known Swiss varieties from the Alps.

Beyond Morteau is **Villers-le-Lac**; the lake part of the name is associated with the start of the long, narrow **Lac de Chaillexon**; you can take trips on the lake from the town. If you do not have time for that trip, make certain you see the astonishing 30 metres high cascade, the **Saut du Doubs**, towards the northern end of the lake. A

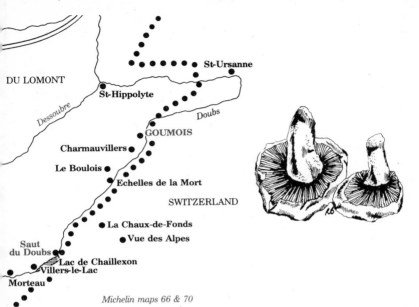

DU LOMONT

St-Ursanne

St-Hippolyte

Dessoubre

Doubs

GOUMOIS

Charmauvillers

Le Boulois

Echelles de la Mort

SWITZERLAND

La Chaux-de-Fonds

Vue des Alpes

Saut
du Doubs

Lac de Chaillexon

Villers-le-Lac

Morteau

Michelin maps 66 & 70

few kilometres downstream is the man-made Barrage du Chatelot, which forms the
northern barrier to this long stretch of water. The lake changes its character totally
in the space of these few kilometres: at Villers-le-Lac it is tranquil enough; at the
Saut du Doubs, where it shoots forth its amazing cascade, it is a narrow strip of
foaming water trapped by steep walls of rock. An unmarked road takes you to
within 200 metres of the cascade – follow the signs.

At this point it would be best to retrace your steps to Villers-le-Lac and make the
crossing into Switzerland. **La Chaux-de-Fonds** is famous throughout the world –
again for watchmaking skills; to the south-east is the equally famous viewpoint
called the **Vue des Alpes** – on a clear day it provides one of the most extensive
panoramas of the Swiss Alps that you'll find.

Use the D464 after recrossing the Franco/Swiss border on the River Doubs north
of La Chaux-de-Fonds; to the north of the river crossing is the unusual natural sight
called the **Echelles de la Mort**. It's best seen from a viewpoint lost amongst thick
woods and high above the narrow, rocky gorge; use the track off the D292 at **Le
Boulois** and walk the last few hundred metres – it's a spectacular scene. Make the
effort to see it.

Before completing the next stage of your drive to Goumois, stop at **Charmauvillers**; here is one of the countless *fromageries* in the Jura where, in the morning,
you can see **Comté** cheese being made. **Comté** is a Gruyère cheese – the huge disks
weigh between 40 and 50 kilograms. It is used to make two local specialities; the
renowned *fondue*, and *gougère* – a savoury cheese pastry. Both the cheese, and
cream, feature in many local specialities, including chicken dishes, soups and a host

73

of *gratins*. Mountain hams are commonplace hereabouts, as is a dish called *caquelon de morilles à la creme* – *caquelon* is the name of the dish in which the morels (edible, dark, honeycombed wild mushrooms) are cooked. It goes without saying that trout features strongly on all restaurant menus.

Breathe in the invigorating mountain air of Goumois and revel in the utter seclusion of this verdant corner of France and Switzerland. Cross the border on the river to Switzerland and recross the Doubs again to **St-Ursanne** – you'll still be in Switzerland, as this is a corner of the countryside where the Doubs flows through Swiss hills and forests. All this terrain is at its best in September when the pastures are carpeted with the lilac-coloured autumn crocus. The woods, too, are an inspiration – the mix of pines and deciduous trees are an additional enticement; you will want to linger long in this glorious country.

Finish your exploration of this first river by following its northern bank back into France and on to **St-Hippolyte**, where the tiny Dessoubre joins the mighty Doubs; of special interest in the town are its 17th century houses. Far to the west, 30 kilometres before the Doubs reaches **Besançon**, there is another small section of the river which is worth seeking out: both the small town of **Baume-les-Dames**; and the countryside across on the southern side of the Doubs – principally, the road that follows the tiny stream called the **Cusancin** up to its source, the Source Bleue. On your way from St-Hippolyte to Baume-les-Dames, you skirt the **Montagnes du Lomont**; navigate through the narrow lanes to a handsome château at **Belvoir** – it offers extensive views southwards from its site.

In the second part of this chapter let us look at what the tiny river called the

Saut du Doubs: where the river falls over 30 metres

The abbey park at the Cirque de Consolation: a wonderland of springs and streams

Dessoubre has to offer. From the point it joins the Doubs – at St-Hippolyte – you can follow its banks every kilometre of the way right up to its source. I promise you that each and every one of those 33 kilometres you drive will be completely satisfying and will provide quiet, happy pleasure. You'll just want to stop as often as you can to fill your eyes with delightful scenes – your subconscious mind will store those attractive images away so that you can recall them in the years to come.

The source of the Dessoubre provides a spectacular end to your journey. Enjoy first the abbey park; a wonderland of springs, streams, trees and woods. But then make the short drive up the steep sides of the **Cirque de Consolation** (*cirque* means *amphitheatre* – in this case, of hills) to the remarkable viewpoint called the **Roche du Prêtre** – where below you is one of the most pleasing sights in all the Jura hills. Once again you'll want to linger long in this exquisite corner of France, ignored by the vast majority of tourists. Their loss is your gain.

It was in the neighbourhood of this lonely spot that I discovered for myself how helpful some French people can be. A simple thing like the loss of a throttle return spring on my car had left me in trouble; the first passing motorist stopped – then promptly drove over 30 kilometres, there and back, to a garage to get a suitable spring for me. On your travels you will come across many examples of kindness; equally, you will also see how contrary some French folk can be. The worst examples I've encountered have been at the best of hotels and restaurants, where minimal effort was made to help other clients who had little knowledge of French. The French can be an enigma; surprisingly, they were voted by North American travel writers as a nation of people that are as unfriendly as Russians and Iranians!

75

The only answer is for you to meet them at least half way; make an effort to understand some of the language and to master some of the cuisine terms. It was this objective that made me design my book *French Leave* in the way that I did – to help you acquire some of the necessary knowledge to make things easier for you. I hope it achieves that objective.

The final and third part of this chapter explores the Loue Valley. Its source is 15 kilometres to the north of Pontarlier; there is no more spectacular place in the Jura, or indeed in the various French mountain ranges, where you can see a river spring to life. The source is a great cavern where, at its mouth, a splendid *show* of water cascades over rocks; naturally, it is at its best in spring or after periods of heavy rain.

Do not fail to follow the Loue to the point where the Lison joins it (see the chapter called *Jura*); a series of both man-made and natural attractions await you. First the charming villages of **Mouthier-Haute-Pierre** and **Lods**; then **Ornans** with its riverside houses, old buildings, museum, church and riverside views. The *kirsch* made in this valley rivals that of Alsace. Then follows 30 kilometres of pretty river country. One third of the way down this section, at **Cléron**, there is a fine 14th century château, that reflects its superb towers in the waters of the Loue (the Michelin map shows other *miroirs*).

There is no better way of finishing your exploration of this lovely corner of France than by relishing the solitude and pastoral charms of this small bit of river country; it's a perfect example of the special benefits that the area keeps for visitors who seek them out – woods, pastures and quiet river valleys, from the mighty Doubs to the minute Dessoubre.

North of Goumois: typical green, quiet Doubs terrain

CIRQUE DE CONSOLATION   Faivre
Simple rest. with rooms (no showers or baths)/Secluded

It was Jean Robertson of *The Sunday Times* who first led me here nearly 20 years ago – the surrounding countryside is sheer heaven. The restaurant part is built on stilts and it sits beside a small waterfall. Relish the wonderland of the nearby abbey park; trees, springs and streams to enchant you. Relish also the *brési beurre*, *jambon fumé du pays* and *morilles* with various dishes.
fpm A–B *meals* NC *rooms* 10 A *closed* Nov. Dec. Tues (out of season).
post Cirque de Consolation. 25390 Orchamps-Vennes. Doubs. *phone* (81) 43.55.38.

FUANS   Patton
Simple hotel/Quiet/Terrace

A small *Logis de France* in a minute hamlet well placed for excursions into Switzerland and for you to explore all the best of the River **Doubs** country – be particularly sure to see the spectacular **Saut du Doubs** (a road takes you very close to it). The usual Jura culinary pleasures feature strongly: *jambon de montagne*, *truites* (prepared in various ways) and *morilles* in several dishes.
fpm A–B *meals* NC *rooms* 10 A–C *closed* Nov. Fri evg and Sat midday (Oct–May).
post Fuans. 25390 Orchamps-Vennes. Doubs. *phone* (81) 43.51.01.

MONTBENOIT   Bon Repos
Simple hotel/Secluded/Terrace/Gardens

A charming *Logis de France* and *Relais du Silence* high above the village with its famous abbey; a bonus are the fine views across the **Doubs** Valley. Ignore the single railway line – just two small trains pass by each day. The hotel is well placed for this area, the *Jura* to the south and nearby Switzerland. *Jésus de Morteau, poulet au vin jaune aux morilles* and *omelette Norvégienne* are delicious.
fpm A–C *meals* C *rooms* 22 B–C *closed* Oct–Apl.
post 25650 Montbenoît. Doubs. *phone* (81) 38.10.77.

PONT-LES-MOULINS   Levant
Comfortable hotel/Gardens

An unpretentious, dull-looking place but surprisingly well fitted out bedrooms and with anything but a dull reputation as far as cooking is concerned. *Truites, jambon fumé, Jésus de Morteau, cassolette d'escargots*, many good Jura cheeses and *morilles* in various dishes appear on the menus. Be sure to enjoy the tiny **Cusancin** Valley up to its source, the Source Bleue.
fpm A–D *meals* NC *rooms* 15 B–D *closed* Nov–Feb.
post Pont-les-Moulins. 25110 Baume-les-Dames. Doubs. *phone* (81) 84.09.99.

13

BARBOTAN-LES-THERMES ●

Fourcès ●

Montréal ●

Larressingle

● VILLENEUVE-DE-MARSAN

◀ LANDES

Adour

● Nogaro
● LUPPE-VIOLLES

● AIRE-SUR-L'ADOUR

●
EUGÉNIE-LES-BAINS
● RISCLE
St-Mont

● PLAISANCE
●
Madiran ●
Beaumarchés
Bassoue
●
Marciac

Pau ↓

Michelin maps 79 & 82

Gers is a *département* in Gascony – a truly delightful pastoral corner of France. I always find it quite amazing that guide book after guide book conveniently ignores this superb area, full of satisfying scenic pleasures and incomparable gastronomic treats. No wonder many of the great chefs who exercise their talents within its confines repeatedly ask why so few people visit it, to try those culinary delights on the spot, rather than consume them back home in other parts of the world. More about that later – but I'm going to do my bit to ensure that you, too, don't miss Gers; I implore you to set aside a few days to enjoy its many attractions.

This part of Gascony is full of green, rolling hills, interlaced with pretty, tranquil valleys, most of which run south to north; the main rivers all rise in the majestic Pyrénées far to the south. There's only one town of any size – **Auch**; it has one exceptional treasure which you must see – the Cathédrale Ste-Marie with its magnificent choir stalls – amongst the finest to be found in Europe – and equally fascinating stained-glass windows.

If your interests are architecturally inclined I must admit that there is not a great deal for you to see in Gers; let me locate what there is and then turn my attention to its other delights. I am a great fan of **Condom**; the route from Auch to Condom can take you past the interesting 12th-century **Abbaye de Flaran**. Condom is handsomely sited above and alongside the River **Baïse**. The market town has a Gothic cathedral with fine cloisters, old streets and an **Armagnac** museum – I talk more about that noble brandy later. The Table des Cordeliers is a fairly expensive, and famous, restaurant; it's worth the financial sacrifice to both eat there and enjoy the unusual sight of the most stunning conversion I've seen in France – a restaurant

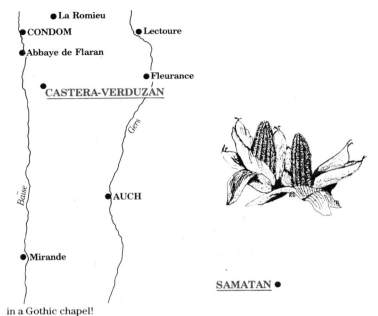

in a Gothic chapel!

Just east of Condom is the tiny *cité* of **La Romieu** – with its college and two excellent examples of Gascony towers. Further east is **Lectoure**, sitting high above the River **Gers**; it's a super site with attractive promenades and pretty views to the west over the river. There is also an interesting museum and cathedral.

Before you leave the general area of Condom and Auch, I would certainly urge you to seek out several of the *bastides* (fortified towns) in Gers. All of them were built 600 to 700 years ago by both the Kings of England and of France. Most have a common design: rectangular in shape with fortified walls and streets – within the walls – which all run at right-angles to each other. In the centre is a fortified church and, nearby, a main square with covered arcades.

South of Lectoure is **Fleurance** – one of the larger French *bastides*; in the last few years it has won world-wide publicity as the starting point for the Tour de France cycle race – the citizens of the small town paid a heavy price for the pleasure, considering it worthwhile for the publicity value.

South-west of Auch, at the point the main N21 crosses the River Baïse, is **Mirande**, one of the biggest *bastides* and again French built. But I suspect the three really small examples west of Mirande will interest you even more: **Bassoues**, with its remarkable *donjon* (keep); **Beaumarchés**; and **Marciac** (the first two are on the road to **Plaisance**). Finally, there remain three fascinating examples just west of Condom – don't miss them. Like all the others I have listed, **Montréal** was built by the French – it has a *perched* site. The only English example is just to the north, at **Fourcès**; a minute, *circular* bastide – it's really fantastic – don't miss it. Also visit the smallest of all French fortified villages at Larressingle

You'll find other interesting, ancient man-made sites throughout the *département* – but what of the scenic sights that Mother Nature has fashioned? You'll see splendid trees, at their best in the north-west corner surrounding the captivating, small spa of **Barbotan-les-Thermes**. All the woods hereabouts have varieties of deciduous trees; further west, beyond the left-hand edge of my map, are the pine forests of the **Landes**. Detour west to see, and smell, these, the largest man-made forests in France; bordered on the west by the Atlantic.

Equally, you'll be fascinated by the visual sights in the hills and valleys between **Aire-s-l'Adour** and **Pau**. Rural France, particularly in April, is at its most alluring; the eyes filled by the shades of the newly-turned browns of ploughed fields, interwoven with emerald meadows and the new tints of lime, sand, yellow and green spring foliage of the plane trees, the chestnuts, the poplars and the willows. **Eugénie-les-Bains** is a classic example; Michel Guérard, one of the best and most famous chefs in France, weaves his magic at his hotel Les Prés et Les Sources d'Eugénie in this tiny hamlet. It is possible you will not be able to afford to eat there; but don't let that stop you driving in. Don't be afraid to do this – blame me if you're questioned! In spring the grounds provide the surprises that only France, at that time of year, can offer: primroses, daffodils, tulips, bluebells, lilacs and roses; amazingly all flowering together.

Now head east again towards Plaisance. From the hills before you reach the River **Adour** come superb examples of local French wines. The vineyards surrounding **Madiran** produce a marvellous red wine that has the same name as the village; from

Larressingle: a handsomely restored fortified *gem*

The circular *bastide* at Fourcès: don't pass it by

the same general area comes the amusingly-named sweet, golden-coloured wine, **Pacherenc du Vic-Bilh** – often described on menus as **Vic-Bilh**. From the hills near Eugénie come the red and white wines of **Tursan**. North of Madiran are the unknown wines of the **Côtes de St-Mont**, rapidly making a name for themselves. Try them all – rather than ordering more expensive clarets.

In your travels throughout the western half of this rich, arable area of France, you will see a great number of vines; from these are harvested, in vast quantities, grapes which are made into white wine and then, as a second stage, distilled to make the oldest of French brandies, **Armagnac**. It is a superb after-dinner liqueur; all the chefs in this part of the world, quite rightly, promote it very strongly indeed. Its champion supporters are three of the best chefs in France: Maurice Coscuella at his hotel La Ripa Alta in Plaisance; André Daguin at the Hôtel de France in Auch; and Roger Duffour at the Relais de l'Armagnac at **Luppé-Violles**. They all possess an astonishing ability to taste a range of Armagnac brandies and then identify both their place and year of birth. Maurice, and all the other chefs, will show you how to savour it at its best: cradle your glass in your hands, warm the contents for some minutes, relish the comforting warmth that the brandy gives your whole being and finally, breathe in the differing perfumes the various types of Armagnac release. Relish them often, as I have done – but beware also over-indulgence; the consequences during the next day can be painful!

What of the pleasures of the table? Well Armagnac plays another part in one of the specialities of the region – bottled fruits macerated in the brandy will often be seen in shop windows: prunes, raspberries, cherries (*griottes*), plums and so on.

Those same fruits, grown in the *départements* of Gers and its neighbours, are made into jams. But the best known specialities are *foie gras* (goose liver), *foie de canard* (duck liver) and *confit* (that means *preserved* – both goose and duck). Throughout the hills and valleys you will pass countless farmyards where geese and ducks have the freedom to waddle and wander where they wish – later to be fattened and used for those splendid specialities. Quite different sorts of speciality are appetisers frequently served before you start a meal; *grattons* – a mixture of small pieces of rendered down pork fat (scratchings) and *graisserons* – made the same way from duck and goose fat. They are so tasty one tends to tuck in with a vengeance – but, beware again – they are really filling and you could find yourself unable to eat even the first course! Finally, enjoy locally-caught salmon from the Adour.

For the sporting enthusiast there are many attractions. Fishing can be enjoyed in many of the streams; shooting, too, is rewarding in the numerous woods of the *département*. Rugby is a flourishing sport in the south-west – its supporters are fanatical enthusiasts; at all levels, from schoolboys to international players, the sport is played with great flair and verve. If you have the opportunity, try to see a game. Motor sport enthusiasts have the chance to enjoy motor racing on one of the few town circuits in France, at Pau; there is also a flourishing *unknown* track at **Nogaro**, north-east of Aire-s-l'Adour. Though Pau lies to the south of the *département* of Gers, do not fail to give it some of your time. I write about it in the chapter called *Pyrénées – Western*; few people know that Pau was the site of the first golf course to be built in Europe – it was opened over 125 years ago. That's just one of its many alluring facets.

Unknown Nogaro: Renault testing their F1 Turbo (author's prerogative!)

AIRE-SUR-L'ADOUR   Commerce
Comfortable restaurant with rooms/Gardens/GC

Of the 100 entries in this book the Commerce has the least quiet site; it is essential you ask for *une chambre tranquille*; this shortcoming is more than made up for by an excellent reputation for good cooking; *civet de canard au Madiran* and *omelette aux cèpes* are on the menus. Note that the *French Leave* entries for **Luppé-Violles** and **Plaisance** are marvellous alternatives.

fpm A–C *meals* NC *rooms* 22 A–C *closed* Jan. Mon.
post 3 Rue Labeyrie. 40800 Aire-Sur-l'Adour. Landes. *phone* (58) 76.60.06.

CASTERA-VERDUZAN   Florida-Besant
Simple restaurant with rooms/Terrace

This small, handsome place is in a minute *thermal resort*; as an added bonus it has a tiny terrace, shaded by a chestnut tree. It is an ideal base from which you can explore many of the *bastides*: I implore you not to miss **Fourcès** – built in a circle – and **Larressingle** – the size of two tennis courts. Cuisine much above average; a range of local products predominates.

fpm A–D *meals* NC *rooms* 23 B–C *closed* Oct–Mar. Rest only: Sun evg and Mon.
post 32410 Castéra-Verduzan. Gers. *phone* (62) 28.53.22.

RISCLE   Paix
Simple hotel

A modest, sand-coloured establishment, away from the busy main road that runs through the village. It has a particularly sound reputation with the locals; inevitably it means the produce of Gers takes pride of place on the menus. Without fail try all the many local wines but particularly be certain to enjoy the **Côtes de St-Mont** varieties from the hills to the immediate west.

fpm A–B *meals* C *rooms* 17 A–B *closed* Sept.
post 32400 Riscle. Gers. *phone* (62) 69.70.14.

SAMATAN   Maigné
Simple hotel

Apart from being well recommended by all the guides, I received two letters of commendation for this humble place from *French Leave* readers; they thought it deserved a star. While I'm not sure about that, I'll agree that cooking is good; *soupe de fèves* and *gratin d'endives* are two specialities. The hotel has an unusually-shaped, partly vine-covered façade.

fpm A–C *meals* NC *rooms* 15 A–B *closed* Mid Sept–end Oct.
post 32130 Samatan. Gers. *phone* (62) 62.30.24.

14

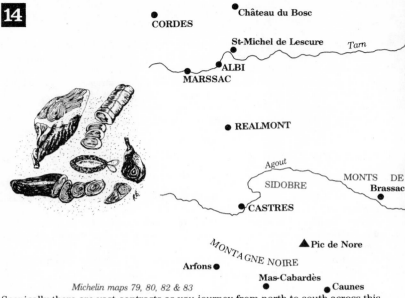

CORDES

●Château du Bosc

St-Michel de Lescure

Tarn

●ALBI
MARSSAC

● REALMONT

Agout

SIDOBRE

MONTS DE
Brassac

●CASTRES

MONTAGNE NOIRE

▲ Pic de Nore

Arfons ●

Mas-Cabardès
●   ●Caunes

Michelin maps 79, 80, 82 & 83

Scenically there are vast contrasts as you journey from north to south across this largely ignored area of France. The northern edges are bordered by the middle reaches of the mighty River **Tarn** – between the two splendid towns of **Millau** and **Albi**; the Tarn Valley here is not as breathtaking and dramatic as the higher reaches, north-east of Millau. To the immediate south of Millau are the rock strewn, barren and rather ugly stretches of plateaux country – called *causses*. The *Cévennes* area demonstrates that the best sights to see in the *causses* are hidden underground – this area, too, has caves in the north-east corner whose hidden delights will please the tastebuds rather than the eyes – but more of that later! Further south are ranges of hills – running in bands from east to west – that are green, cool and surprisingly attractive. Finally, to the south of these hills and on the southern edges of my map you have the dry-looking countryside that forms the coastal plain bordering the Mediterranean; its delights are its wines which will please, once again, senses other than sight.

Let's start in the far north. Millau is one of my favourite small French towns – the gateway to many of Nature's most unusual treasures in France. (See the *Cévennes* chapter for an alternative hotel in Millau.) The Tarn Valley to the west of the town attracts a minimal number of tourists – the lanes that follow its banks are quite deserted. It's not spectacular stuff but there are dozens of interesting viewpoints and spots where you can linger and enjoy the river scenery. Make one detour some 20 kilometres after leaving Millau; to the north of the Tarn is **Castelnau-Pégayrols**, a minute, secluded hamlet with two 900 year old churches. Further downstream is the old *perched* village of **Brousse-le-Château** with its ruined castle.

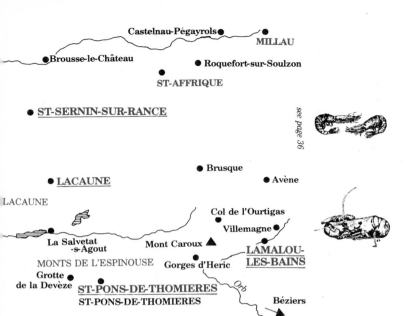

see page 36

Albi, the red-brick town, has many magnificent treasures; the best of them is the glorious cathedral. It, too, is built of red brick – it looks more like a fortress; the interior is superb – full of frescoes and statuary and a fine choir, surrounded by a beautiful stone screen. Toulouse-Lautrec was born in Albi; immediately to the north of the cathedral is the Palais de la Berbie, alongside the Tarn. It houses the most important collection of paintings by the artist. Walk the quiet streets to the east of the cathedral – they are at their best in the cool, quiet hours of dusk. North-east of the town, just five kilometres away and alongside the Tarn, is the 11th century church of **St-Michel de Lescure**.

To the north of Albi are two delightful corners of the *département* of Tarn. The 700 year old fortified hill-top town of **Cordes**, full of old streets with fine Gothic houses, has become a flourishing artistic centre; but be warned – the streets of the town – though rewarding – are both narrow and steep.

The second delight that should fill some of your hours is the Viaur Valley to the north-east of Albi. At the point the N88 crosses the river, leave the main road and enjoy the lanes that follow the stream upriver – pretty, wooded country. Two man-made sites deserve your attention. One will require no effort to find – it's the 460 metres long railway viaduct that spans the valley, constructed at the turn of the century. The second will require navigational effort to locate – the **Château du Bosc**, isolated in green country and associated with the Toulouse-Lautrec family.

In my first paragraph I refer to caves, hidden under the limestone *causses*, that house not scenic pleasures, but those of another sort – fit to tempt the tastebuds of any cheese lover. At **Roquefort-sur-Soulzon**, one of the greatest cheeses in the world is produced; it's those hidden caves that provide the special conditions (said to be the best refrigeration sites in the world) that allow the blue mould to form which gives the exquisite blue cheese, made from ewe's milk, such a rare and unusual taste. Over 15,000 tonnes of **Roquefort** cheese ripen every year in the caves in the neighbourhood of the town; the ewe's milk comes from all over southern France. Throughout the country – and in other parts of the world – there are many imitations of this salty, three star special; locally you will find **Bleu des Causses** – stored in the same sort of caves under the *causses* circling Millau, but, and an important difference, it's a cheese made from cow's milk. A few kilometres to the west of Roquefort is the ancient town of **St-Affrique** – well worth a visit.

Castres is a modest enough place – it has two attractions worth seeking out: the Goya Museum which has many fine examples of that talented artist's work; and the houses alongside the river **Agout**. But it is the marvellous country to the east that is my cup of tea; a series of delightful hills stretch eastwards in a narrow band, all of them being north of the main N112 that runs south-east to **Béziers** from Castres. Ignore that main road and head for those hills.

The first small circle of country nearest Castres is called the Sidobre; its border to the north is the River Agout and within its wooded hills are some of the strangest quirks of Nature you'll ever see. All sorts of weird granite rocks lie hidden amongst the trees – the most unusual is the amusingly-named Peyro-Clabado, like a Centurion tank sitting on top of a Mini. Amongst other formations in the Sidobre are the Rocher de Sept-Faux and the *chaos* immediately adjacent to the Grotte St-Dominique. Do search these and others out; it is all most unusual terrain – you won't

86   South of St-Sernin-sur-Rance: enjoy the local *chèvre* cheeses

be disappointed.

The Sidobre is the western border of the Haut Languedoc Regional Nature Park and most of the countryside I describe in these final paragraphs lies within its boundaries. The next circle of country that sits to the east of the Sidobre is called the Monts de Lacaune. I can still recall the first time I saw these green, cool hills in late April. They came as such a surprise after the dry, rocky hills to the north of Narbonne. I have wanted to return for many years; the research for this book allowed me to go back and relish again the same delight.

Three pleasant small towns ring the circle of hills; **Brassac**, **Lacaune** and **La Salvetat-s-Agout**. All of them are perfect examples of what life is like in the rural communities of France, unseen by most tourists. It's in dozens of places like these, throughout France, where you see the country's real strength and where you appreciate its immense agricultural importance. As a bonus to these towns there are attractive lakes to the east and west of La Salvetat and, south of Lacaune is a fine viewpoint that lies at an altitude in excess of 1200 metres. The area is renowned for its excellent *charcuterie*.

South and east of La Salvetat-s-Agout, and to the north of the rivers Jaur and **Orb**, is another small group of hills known by the name Monts de l'Espinouse. I was just as much captivated by these wooded hills and pastures as their cousins to the north. These hills fall steeply down to **St-Pons**. This is a splendid small place with an ancient church and it houses the central office for the Regional Park. Nearby, to the immediate west, is the **Grotte de la Devèze** with fine examples of stalagmites and stalactites. To the north-east, near the point where the Jaur and Orb join, are the **Gorges d'Heric**, a dramatic sight where the torrent falls steeply from the heights of **Mont Caroux**; you can reach them by car along a narrow road that gets you quite close – but you must walk the last stretches upwards.

Lamalou-les-Bains is a small spa, long famous for its waters. It makes a splendid base to explore all the countryside detailed in earlier paragraphs and, in addition, the scenic roads that abound to the north. One thoroughly enjoyable round trip would be via the D180, over the **Col de l'Ourtigas**, to its junction with the D922. Drive north to **Brusque** and then, in a semicircle to the east, to **Avène** and its nearby man-made lake. Follow the Orb Valley back towards Lamalou-les-Bains, making a short detour via **Villemagne**.

The final bit of country that makes this area so scenically interesting is the forbiddingly-named **Montagne Noire**; it's south of Castres and forms the natural barrier between that town and Carcassonne – it, too, is also part of the Haut Languedoc Regional Nature Park. The northern slopes of this hilly barrier are covered by similar vegetation to that seen in the Monts de Lacaune; its southern flanks have a Mediterranean flavour about them, where the vine and olive flourish. Use all the mountain roads that climb up through the forests between Castres and **Arfons** and then head east, to the other side of the main D118 road: the 1210 metres high **Pic de Nore**, with its TV mast and splendid viewpoint; and the ancient village of **Mas-Cabardès**; are two important detours you must make. On the southern slopes to the south-east of the Montagne Noire are the famed marble quarries near **Caunes** and the numerous vineyards of **Minervois** – really excellent dry red wines are made from the grapes you'll see growing there.

88   Peyro-Clabado in the Sidobre: like a Centurion tank sitting on a Mini!

LACAUNE
Hôtel Fusiès

Comfortable hotel/Terrace

Lacaune is 800 metres above sea-level. Its buildings all have grey slate roofs; they remind one of Wales – as do many of the scenic views surrounding the town. A warm, welcoming hotel with a wide range of good-value menus: *soupe de montagne, jambon* and *charcuterie de Lacaune* (the town is famous for it), *truites* and *omelèttes* (both the latter prepared in many different ways) will please you.
fpm A–D *meals* C *rooms* A–C *closed* Mid Dec–end Jan. Sun evg (Nov–Feb).
post Rue République, 81230 Lacaune. Tarn. *phone* (63) 37.02.03.

LAMALOU-LES-BAINS
Belleville

Comfortable hotel/Terrace/Gardens/Lift

A smart place with a shady terrace in this tiny spa town. Lamalou allows you to explore both Haut Languedoc and the *Cévennes* – it also has the big bonus of being about one hour's drive from the Mediterranean. Specialities have a strong smell of various seas – dishes like *gigot de mer, gambas grillées, filet de hareng* and *brandade de morue*. There's a wide variety of Languedoc wines.
fpm A–C *meals* NC *rooms* 44 A–D *closed* Open all the year.
post 34240 Lamalou-les-Bains. Hérault. *phone* (67) 95.61.09.

ST-PONS-DE-THOMIERES
Aub. du Cabaretou

Comfortable restaurant with rooms/Quiet

This light lime-coloured *auberge* is amongst the woods at the summit of the Col du Cabaretou, high above St-Pons – and 10 kilometres from the town. Inevitably there are extensive views as you look south. There are both simple and ambitious dishes on the menus: *jambon cru de nos montagnes* (from the hills to the north), *tarte aux cèpes et aux noix* and *cassolette de rognons et ris de veau*.
fpm B–D *meals* C *rooms* 10 A–D *closed* Mid–end Sept. Feb. Wed (Oct–Mar).
post 34220 St-Pons-de-Thomières. Hérault. *phone* (67) 97.02.31.

ST-SERNIN-SUR-RANCE
France

Simple hotel/Terrace

A smart *Logis de France* surrounded by marvellous green countryside – extensive views will be yours if you go west or south from the town. Cuisine has strong ties with the produce of the region; *terrines du Rouergue* (the area around Rodez – to the north), *jambon de pays* and a *sélection spéciale* of the superb and incomparable **Roquefort** cheeses (be certain to visit the caves there).
fpm A–C *meals* NC *rooms* 20 A–C *closed* Sun evg and Mon (Nov–Easter).
post 12380 St-Sernin-sur-Rance. Aveyron. *phone* (65) 99.60.26.

JURA

15

Arc-et-Senans ● *Lison*

● Salins-les-Bains

Levier ●

Pontarlier ●

Arbois ●

● Cirque du Fer à Cheval

● Poligny

Forêt de la Joux

Doubs

Lac de Saint Point

PASSENANS
●

MALBUISSON
MALBUISSON ●

● Cirque de Ladoye

Le Morond ▲

ST-GERMAIN-LES-ARLAY
●

Le Mont d'Or ▲

● Château-Châlon

Champagnole ●

● Nozeroy

● Baume-les-Messieurs

● Cirque de Baume

Cascade de la Billaude ●

Lons-le-Saunier
●

CHATILLON ●

Lac de Chalain

Ilay ●

Doucier ●

▲ Pic de l'Aigle

Hérisson

SWITZERLAND

Lac de Vouglans

Morez ●

Bienne

Ain

ST-CLAUDE
ST-CLAUDE
●
● Villard-St-Sauveur

Col de la Faucille ●

▲ Mont Rond

DIVONNE-
LES-BAINS

Lac
Léman

Geneva ●
▼

see page 72

see page 24

Michelin map 70

The Jura range of mountains extends from Belfort to Geneva. I've split them into two chapters; this one – which roughly covers the *département* of Jura, and another earlier chapter, *Doubs*, which corresponds approximately to the *département* of the same name (the northern part of the range).

Don't think of the Jura mountains as rivals of the Alps; the highest of them rises to no more than 1700 metres. They are lovely hills – thickly wooded with pines, carpeted with green pastures and interlaced with dozens of gurgling streams. As an added bonus there are a few attractive lakes, ranging in size from the tiniest pool to large, man-made sheets of water. Most of the sights that I describe, and encourage you to visit on your travels, are those shaped and fashioned by Mother Nature; how fair and valid that is in these hills, where seclusion, invigorating air and scenic delights are the main attractions. Local wines and many regional cuisine specialities, relying mainly on the rich produce coming from the hills, are other delights to entice you.

Let me start my look at the Jura in the southern section – at the town of St-Claude. It prospered originally, 200 years ago, because of its reputation for making the world's best pipe briars; the town tumbles down from the hills to the floor of the **Bienne** Valley; it's a personal favourite of mine and was much loved by Nevile Shute. There's a pipe museum and a fine Gothic cathedral to add to your interest. View the town from the D304 that climbs to the east; on your ascent you'll pass a spectacular cascade called the Queue de Cheval.

To the west of the town is the River **Ain**. At many points along its length, before it joins the Rhône, it has been made to work for its living; there are several man-made lakes, built in modern times, to harness the power-creating waters of the Jura. The **Lac de Vouglans** is the largest – use the minor roads on its banks to take you to a number of good viewpoints.

To the east of St-Claude, and on the other side of a long ridge of wooded summits that form the eastern escarpment of the Jura, is a small pocket of France that always seems as though it should be a part of Switzerland. The French border runs to within a few kilometres of the western shore of **Lac Léman** (Lake Geneva). **Divonne-les-Bains** is in that small pocket of countryside – and is just six kilometres from the lakeside; it's a handsome, small spa town, much favoured by the Swiss – probably because of its casino, one of the most successful in France. There is a good golf course behind the town on the slopes of the hills, and to the eastern side of the spa is a man-made lake that offers water sports attractions of all kinds. High above Divonne, at the **Col de la Faucille**, is the magnificent viewpoint of **Mont-Rond**

Both to the north and south of St-Claude are the sort of pleasures I enjoy most – endless twisty lanes taking you up and down pine-clad hills and along dramatic, narrow river valleys. The most interesting of these latter sights is the Bienne Valley; use the road that runs along the western side of the Gorges de la Bienne – the D126 eventually brings you to **Morez**.

This town, too, prospered 200 years ago, when it became famous for the production of spectacle frames. An absorbing diversion at Morez is to take a short train ride to the north to Morbier – you'll be fascinated to discover how the line rises high above the town through tunnels and across viaducts.

92   Cirque de Baume: an example of the resurgent Jura springs (Les Reculées)

The central part of this area lies in the triangle that has Morez, **Champagnole** and **Lons-le-Saunier** at its three extremities. The very centre of the triangle is known as the Région des Lacs; half a dozen or so small lakes that form the **Hérisson** Valley. Before you explore it, view it from a fine viewpoint to the east, the **Pic de l'Aigle** – it's a good invigorating walk to the summit. The highlights of the Hérisson Valley, from **Ilay** to **Doucier**, are the two dozen or more cascades; the river falls over 250 metres in three kilometres and in wet weather the sight of the rushing water, shooting down the narrow valley, is a memorable one. The biggest of the lakes is north of Doucier – **Lac de Chalain**; swimming and boating facilities are available here. It's all lovely country.

In the hills north-east of Lons-le-Saunier are various delightful spots to include on your travels. Two of these were sculptured by natural means; the **Cirque de Baume** and the **Cirque de Ladoye**. These *amphitheatres* should be seen from both the valley floors and the roads that climb to the top of their rocky walls. **Baume-les-Messieurs**, a tiny village in the valley floor below the *cirque*, is a special delight. It was from the 6th century abbey here, founded by the Irish Saint Colomban, that a dozen monks went west to establish the abbey at Cluny. (*France à la Carte* tells you the story of the abbeys of France.) Drive to the head of the valley and marvel at the pretty spectacle of an unusual small waterfall.

Château-Châlon is a few kilometres to the north – sitting high above the village of Voiteur. You'll get splendid views from its site; it has become more famous, however, for its *vin jaune*, a rare wine, deep yellow, very dry and made from the Savagnin (Traminer) grape. An excellent chicken dish, using this wine, is a speciality of the area. Before finally leaving this central section spare some time for Lons-le-Saunier; the old arcades of the Rue du Commerce, churches and a museum are amongst its treasures.

The third and final part of this area of the Jura is the countryside between **Arbois** in the west, **Pontarlier** on the eastern border with Switzerland, and Champagnole to the south. Let's start near Champagnole.

The narrow roads that follow both the infant River Ain and a tributary, the Saine, show off typical Jura scenery at its best. Near the junction of those two streams is the **Cascade de la Billaude**. Close to the source of the Ain is the *lost* fortified medieval village of **Nozeroy** – seek it out.

North-east of Champagnole is one of the greatest pleasures of the entire Jura range – the **Forêt de la Joux**. Despite its 6,000 acres, it's not the largest pine forest in France, but surely it must be the finest. Lose yourself in its depths; there is a signposted route – Route des Sapins – through the forest from Champagnole to **Levier** (on the D72 west of Pontarlier). It passes a series of interesting spots; including an arboretum and the truly magnificent Sapin Président – a specimen pine tree with a circumference of four metres (it requires a longish walk to reach it).

A few kilometres west of Levier is the source of the River **Lison**. Don't miss it; like the Loue (see the *Doubs* chapter), it *rises* from the mouth of a cave. Also seek out the adjoining Grotte Sarrazine.

Arbois is the small town where Pasteur worked for so long. It's famous also for *rosé* and sparkling white wines (*vin fou – mad* wine); there is also a version of the *vin jaune*, mentioned earlier, made in the nearby vineyards. But the truly splendid scenic treasures are just a few kilometres away to the south-east; the **Cirque du Fer à Cheval** and the Reculée des Planches. Drive the roads that all but encircle these two natural sights; the *cirque* is a typical example of a Jura-type amphitheatre of wooded rock faces. The River Cuisance has two sources: the Petite Source de la Cuisance; and the Grande Source de la Cuisance – the latter is a thrilling sight, particularly in wet weather. Explore the Grottes des Planches at the Grande Source (resurgent streams cascading over rocks).

South of Arbois is **Poligny**, an ancient town with interesting architectural sights: the Hôtel-Dieu, churches and the old Grande Rue. North-east of Arbois is **Salins-les-Bains**, a spa town where salt has been mined since pre-Roman times; you can still see the underground mines. Nearby is the equally interesting *salt* town of **Arc-et-Senans**, where you can visit the few buildings that remain from what was going to be an 18th century planned town – La Saline Royale.

South of Pontarlier, on the upper stretches of the River **Doubs**, is the **Lac de Saint Point**. Legend has it that the deep waters of the lake cover an old and prosperous town; it's said the town refused shelter to a mother and her child and its punishment was to be flooded for evermore. It is a calm place; surrounded by wooded hills, and with roads that encircle the lake, it offers all sorts of added interests that will please both adults and children alike: bathing facilities, boating and other water sports opportunities. Search out the source of the Doubs to the south of the lake and make the climb to viewpoints on **Le Mont d'Or** and **Le Morond** – views of the Jura mountains, Swiss lakes, and the Alps in the far east, will be your reward.

Cirque du Fer à Cheval: from the D469 that climbs its western wall

MALBUISSON
Les Terrasses

Comfortable hotel/Terrace/Gardens

A modern, whitewashed, chalet-type *Logis de France* – overlooking the calm **Lac de St-Point**, it's an ideal spot for enjoying the River **Doubs** country and for hopping across the border into Switzerland. *Morilles* feature in various dishes like *poulet aux morilles* and *escalope aux morilles*; other offerings include *pâté en croûte, truite au bleu* and *pêche Melba*
fpm A–D *meals* NC *rooms* 26 C–D *closed* Mar. Nov–Jan. Mon (out of season).
post 25160 Malbuisson. Doubs. *phone* (81) 89.30.24.

PASSENANS
Revermont

Comfortable hotel/Secluded/Gardens/Swimming pool/Lift

A modern, unattractive building in large grounds at the northern entrance to a charming village. The Revermont is a *Relais du Silence*; as a bonus it's surrounded by fine wine country – buy some from the merchants in the village. Cooking is modest – amongst the specialities are *terrine de poisson, truite au bleu, tourte de volaille aux noisettes* and *poulet de Bresse à l'Arbois*.
fpm A–B *meals* C *rooms* 28 A–D *closed* Jan. Feb. Sun evg and Mon midday (out of season). *post* Passenans. 39230 Sellières. Jura. *phone* (84) 44.61.02.

ST-CLAUDE
Au Retour de la Chasse

Simple hotel/Quiet/Tennis

In an attractive site at **Villard-St-Sauveur**, which is a few kilometres south of St-Claude (not far from the Hôtel Joly, mentioned in *French Leave*). It's a handsome, modern, chalet-style hotel. Jura wines are incorporated into two dishes on the menus: *truite meunière au Côtes de Jura blanc* and *poularde de Bresse au vin d'Arbois blanc*. Another treat is the local *omelette Jurassienne*.
fpm A–B *meals* C *rooms* 12 B–C *closed* Apl. Dec. Sun evg and Mon (except July–Aug). *post* Villard-St-Sauveur. 39200 St-Claude. Jura. *phone* (84) 45.11.32.

ST-GERMAIN-LES-ARLAY
Host. Saint-Germain

Simple hotel/Quiet/Gardens

An unusual stone building with dark green shutters; it's in the village well away from the N83 bypass which skirts it to the west. Be sure to explore nearby **Château-Châlon**, just a few kilometres to the east; magnificent and expensive wines come from the few vineyards on the slopes below the village there. Enjoy *pigeon de Bresse, poulet sauce au vin blanc* and fine Jura cheeses (particularly Morbier).
fpm A–B *meals* C *rooms* 10 B–D *closed* Oct. Tues (out of season).
post 39210 Saint-Germain-lès-Arlay. Jura. *phone* (84) 44.60.91.

MONTS DE LA MADELEINE & DU FOREZ

16

● St-Pourçain

SAIL-LES-BAINS ●

● **Lapalisse**

● **La Pacaudière**

Le Crozet ●

see page 18

Loire

Châtel-Montagne ● **Ambierle**
●

MOLLES
●

Vichy ●

MONTS
DE LA MADELEINE

Busset ●

St-Haon-le-Châtel
●

Barrage de la Tache ●

ROANNE

Les Grands Murcins ●
Rocher de Rochefort ▲

● Renaison

RIORGES

La Loge-des-Gardes ●

St-Alban-
les-Eaux ●

● Villerest

● Châteldon

Gué de la Chaux

● Cascade du Creux-Saillant

St-Maurice-s-Loire ●

Credogne

Les Bois Noirs

● St-Just-en-Chevalet

Cervières
●

● Château d'Urfé

● **Thiers**

Pommiers
●

● Noirétable

Balbigny ●

● Ravel

VOLLORE-MONTAGNE

La Bastie-d'Urfé ●

Allier

● Billom
● Mauzun

● Augerolles

MONTS

DU FOREZ

**MONTROND-
LES-BAINS** ●

Dore

● Busséol

Champdieu ●

● Vic-le-Comte
COMTE

● Job

● Montbrison

● Buron

Col des Supeyres

● Issoire

● **AMBERT**

● Nonette

Michelin map 239

I am well aware how few visitors to France really get off the beaten track: this area, I am absolutely certain, will be known to precious few tourists – and even fewer will have visited it. It is totally unspoilt with quiet valleys and vast stretches of dark, wooded hills – places where you can not only breathe fresh air but you'll have all the breathing space you want – you are not likely to see many fellow tourists in these secluded corners.

Let's start by looking at the eastern half of the area – the two ranges of hills called the **Monts de la Madeleine** and the **Monts du Forez** and the countryside on their eastern flanks. The Monts de la Madeleine are hills to the west of **Roanne**; running from north to south, they reach a height of approximately 1000 or so metres. Before driving up into them and later into those of Forez, to the immediate south – set aside plenty of time to explore a number of villages which lie in the **Loire** Valley at the foot of their eastern slopes.

The first of these villages, **La Pacaudière**, is on the N7 as it cuts south-east towards Roanne and eventually Lyon. One kilometre to the west is tiny **Le Crozet**; it's an old medieval village with a round keep, old houses, a museum and, of particular interest, the interior of the Maison Papon. Return to the N7 and in less than five kilometres bear right to **Ambierle** – another old village with a Gothic church that has magnificent stained glass windows.

On your way to the next highlight, **St-Haon-le-Châtel**, you'll see some vineyards; the **Côte Roannaise** wines are produced from grapes grown there. Try these local wines – you'll enjoy good reds and a renowned *rosé* – the latter frequently being described as a **Renaison** *rosé*. St-Haon-le-Châtel is an ancient fortified village – you can still see part of its walls. Continue south on the D8 and, near **St-Alban-les-Eaux**, make a short detour east to **Villerest**.

It's here that the mighty Loire totally changes its character. From its source far to the south in the Ardèche, it has forced its way through many a gorge; at Roanne it becomes a lazy giant of a river as it flows, first north, and then west, in a huge arc towards the Atlantic. South of Villerest are the last of the dramatic gorges of the Loire; sadly, this stretch of river, upstream towards **Balbigny**, will soon become a man-made lake. Enjoy the countryside straddling the *lake* and particularly spare some time for **St-Maurice-s-Loire**; your reward will be a splendid view of the river valley from its picturesque site.

In the flat terrain south-west of Balbigny – a landscape peppered with *étangs* (meres or pools) – are a handful of treasures you must search out: **Pommiers** is an ancient fortified village with an 11th century Romanesque church; at **La Bastie-d'Urfé** is a Renaissance château partly constructed by Italian artisans – the gardens complement the man-made treasure; finally, at **Champdieu**, north of **Montbrison**, there's a Romanesque church and fortified priory.

From Champdieu you can now head west into the secluded Monts du Forez, losing yourself in the myriad lanes that abound in these dramatic, dark, pine-clad hills; generally head west and then north, finishing your lovely run in the northern range – the Monts de la Madeleine.

To enjoy the best of Forez, perhaps this itinerary would be ideal: aim first for the **Col des Supeyres**; shortly before its summit on the eastern side look out for the fine examples of *jasseries* – the stone-built dairy farms of the Forez where the blue-

98   The old village of Châteldon: on the north-western edge of Les Bois Noirs

veined, tall cylinders of cheese called **Fourme-d'Ambert** are made; they were being made in these hills before Julius Caesar overran Gaul. You will not regret a *deviation* to **Ambert**; nearby, a few kilometres to the east, is an interesting paper mill, the Moulin Richard-de-Bas, where you can see paper being made. From Ambert continue north to **Job**.

A difficult decision has to be made here. Do you return back into the rewarding granite hills of the Forez or do you give some time to the **Dore** Valley? A compromise would be to head downstream following the river, and, near **Augerolles**, climb back into the seclusion of the forests and green pastures.

From Augerolles it's about 20 kilometres or so across the hills to **Noirétable** on the main N89 that runs from Clermont-Ferrand to Lyon. Immediately north of the N89 you re-enter the Monts de la Madeleine; sights nearby include the medieval village of **Cervières** and the ruined **Château d'Urfé** – you reach the latter at the end of a 20-minute walk.

North of **St-Just-en-Chevalet** are a string of attractions. The first is the tiny lake at **Gué de la Chaux** – in the summer a small steam railway runs up to **La Loge-des-Gardes**. Another lake is formed by the **Barrage de la Tache** – drive there via the viewpoint at **Rocher de Rochefort** and allow time for a detour to the arboretum at **Les Grands Murcins** (1,200 trees of many different types). Another attraction is the 12th century church at **Châtel-Montagne**, built in granite quarried from the Auvergne hills. Finish your run at **Lapalisse**, famous for its 15th century château, an amazing conversion of a castle first built 300 years earlier.

The route I am describing has the rough outline of the capital letter *N*; though I realise you could permutate your exploration of the area in many different ways. The third and final part of my route, the left hand stroke of the letter *N*, takes you from Lapalisse, south via **Vichy** and Thiers to **Issoire**.

Vichy is the most famous of all French spa towns; it offers visitors every imaginable facility, and its parks are particularly pleasurable. However, the countryside to the south-east is where I would prefer to head; it hides many a treasure – both scenic and man-made. At **Busset** there's a 500 year old château; at **Châteldon** there are several old, timbered houses. Follow the attractive **Credogne** Valley upstream to the **Cascade du Creux-Saillant** (hidden from the road); beyond the waterfall make sure your drive takes you along the narrow D64 that skirts the southern borders of a lovely piece of country called **Les Bois Noirs** – that name describes its dark, sombre pine woods. Then finish this section by descending into Thiers; marvellously situated, it is full of old timbered houses and has long been famous for the manufacture of knives and scissors.

Your enjoyment of this whole area will be greatly enhanced by the pleasures of the table; meal times or picnics will give you plenty of opportunities to try many of the local wines and cheeses and the specialities of the Auvergne. What are some of these? You will see some vineyards in the Vichy area; these provide the grapes for wines called **Côtes d'Auvergne** – there are several good reds and a fine *rosé*. You'll also come across the Beaujolais-type reds, the Gamays of the **Côtes du Forez** – these come from the area near Montbrison. North of Vichy is **St-Pourçain**; it enjoys an ever increasing and fine reputation for its red wines and a first rate, Loire-type white.

The Loire near St-Maurice-s-Loire: sadly the gorge will soon be flooded

Cheeses will include **Bleu d'Auvergne**, **Murol**, **St-Nectaire** and **Tomme-de-Cantal** – all are made from cow's milk. A goat's milk cheese is **Brique du Forez**, also known as **Chevreton d'Ambert**. *French Leave* describes all these in great detail; be sure to try as many as you can – buy them in the splendid village *fromageries*; nothing could be nicer than buying them locally, when they are always fresh and in superb condition. It is a pleasure I've enjoyed many times.

Regional specialities are countless. You'll come across *potée* – a typical heavy stew of cabbage, vegetables and meat; *tripoux* – sheep's feet cooked in wine and herbs; *aligot* – a purée of potatoes, cheese, garlic and butter; and the many excellent examples of Auvergne *charcuterie* – hams, sausages, *pâtés* and so on. *French Leave* lists many more of them.

Beyond Thiers is the last section of my described route – it contains half a dozen worthwhile places to visit. Start at **Ravel**, where another old castle was converted two centuries ago into a smart château – its terrace, which offers fine views, was designed by Lenôtre. Continue via the ruined castle at **Mauzun**; it must have been a formidable fortress in the days when all its 19 towers were standing. To the south of **Billom** is lovely hill country. It is called **Comté** and **Vic-le-Comte** is at its centre. From the two châteaux at **Buron** and **Busséol** you get vast views of all the surrounding country, including the mountain ranges called Dore and Dômes (extinct volcanoes) to the west. Finish your journey at Issoire with its splendid Eglise St-Austremoine – a Romanesque church built in the 12th century; and, to the south, the ruins of the great fortress of **Nonette**, overlooking the **Allier** with extensive views in all directions.

MOLLES
Relais Fleuri

Comfortable restaurant with rooms/Quiet/Terrace/Gardens/GC

Its name truly does it justice – a small, pretty *Logis de France* just north of the village and on the D62. Two sisters, Jeanne and Suzanne, have won a sound reputation locally for their fine cuisine. A range of ambitious dishes includes amongst them *foie gras de canard, terrine de canard, turbot poché beurre blanc, gratin de fruits de mer* and *pâtisserie maison.*
fpm A–C *meals* C *rooms* 10 A–C *closed* Nov. Dec. Wed.
post Molles. 03300 Cusset. Allier. *phone* (70) 41.80.01.

RIORGES
Le Marcassin

Comfortable restaurant with rooms/Quiet/Terrace

Jean Farge is a highly thought of chef in the vicinity of **Roanne**. His specialities include *rosette de campagne* (Lyonnais sausage), *terrine de ris de veau, feuilleté de homard* and *omble chevalier meunière* (see the chapter called *Chaîne des Aravis*). The modern building is well clear of Roanne, south of the D9 Roanne – **Renaison** road. Good value, good cuisine and quiet site – an attractive combination.
fpm A–C *meals* NC *rooms* 10 B–C *closed* Aug. Feb. Rest only: Sat and Sun (Oct–Apl).
post Riorges. 42300 Roanne. Loire. *phone* (77) 71.30.18.

SAIL-LES-BAINS
Grand Hôtel

Comfortable hotel/Secluded/Gardens/Tennis/Lift

Don't be misled by the impressive sounding name; it's a largish building, built in 1854, lost in the middle of a delightful, wooded park. It's an oasis of charm just north of that horrible highway, the N7; part of a small spa, the thermal baths nestle below the hotel. Cuisine is convential stuff. This is an ideal base to see both this area and the hills of *Beaujolais* to the east.
fpm A–C *meals* NC *rooms* 32 B–E *closed* Mid Sept–mid May.
post Sail-les-Bains. 42310 La Pacaudière. Loire. *phone* (77) 64.30.81.

VOLLORE-MONTAGNE
Touristes

Very simple hotel/Quiet

A green-shuttered, modern building in a tiny hamlet 840 metres above sea-level. There's no shortage of interesting drives that you can make in all directions of the compass – vast stretches of forest everywhere. You'll also see some of those regional dishes I described earlier: *tripoux* and *jambon cru maison* are examples. Also try the Auvergne wines and the many different types of local cheeses.
fpm A–B *meals* C *rooms* 16 A–B *closed* Nov. Mar. Tues evg and Wed (except July–Aug). *post* Vollore-Montagne. 63120 Courpière. Puy-de-Dôme. *phone* (73) 53.77.50.

MORVAN

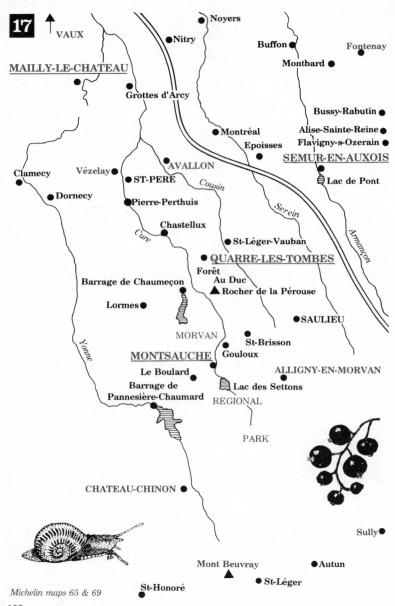

17 ↑ VAUX

Noyers

Nitry

Buffon   Fontenay

Montbard

MAILLY-LE-CHATEAU

Grottes d'Arcy

Bussy-Rabutin

Montréal   Alise-Sainte-Reine

Epoisses   Flavigny-s-Ozerain

SEMUR-EN-AUXOIS

Clamecy   Vézelay   AVALLON   Cousin   Lac de Pont

ST-PÈRE

Dornecy   Pierre-Perthuis   Serein

Chastellux   Cure   Armançon

St-Léger-Vauban

QUARRE-LES-TOMBES

Forêt
Au Duc
Barrage de Chaumeçon   ▲ Rocher de la Pérouse

Lormes   SAULIEU

MORVAN   St-Brisson

MONTSAUCHE   Gouloux   ALLIGNY-EN-MORVAN

Yonne   Le Boulard

Barrage de   Lac des Settons
Pannesière-Chaumard   REGIONAL

PARK

CHATEAU-CHINON

Sully

Mont Beuvray   Autun
▲   St-Léger

St-Honoré

I beg you to set aside some time – even if it's just a couple of days – to explore this delightful area when you next decide to set off for the southern parts of France. Instead of motoring across it at high speed on the autoroute, leave at the first exit you come to in North Burgundy, and then prepare yourself to enjoy a world you probably had no idea existed.

Assuming you take my advice and leave at the **Nitry** exit on the autoroute – your objective will be to use one of my hotel recommendations listed later on or, alternatively, some of those described in *French Leave*. I describe the pleasures of this part of Burgundy on the assumption you travel from the north, criss-crossing the green hills and quiet valleys, finishing somewhere on its southern borders.

At Nitry head due east to **Noyers**. It's a gem of a place, all but surrounded by a loop of the River **Serein**; a small medieval town, much of it is still as it was built 500 years ago. Walk its narrow streets, tiny squares and its walls with their 16 towers. Then head due south along the Serein Valley until you reach **Montréal** – it's a lovely run. Montréal is another 500 year old small town with an impressive site above the river. Explore the church and the narrow streets.

At this point you have a difficult decision; do you head east or west? I suggest you head east first and I'll describe a route that takes you in a big circle eventually bringing you back to nearby **Avallon**.

Aim first for **Montbard** and, if you have the time, enjoy its park, castle and the Canal de Bourgogne. Better still, follow the canal seven kilometres to the north-west, to the restored forge at **Buffon**; from June to September (afternoons only) the Taylor-Whitehead family will welcome you and show you this intriguing ancient monument. Now seek out four special treasures to the east and south-east of Montbard.

The first of them is the abbey at Fontenay , *lost* in the woods to the east of the town. The abbey was founded in 1118 by two of Saint Bernard's uncles – it's a perfect example of the flowering of the Cistercian influence. It was the second *daughter* of the abbey at Clairvaux (70 kilometres to the north-east) and there is no finer place in which to grasp just why Burgundy, the mother of all the arts, became so important. Fontenay remains today in marvellous condition.

Within 20 kilometres is the best of all the Burgundy châteaux: **Bussy-Rabutin** is a delightful, small building with gardens designed by Lenôtre; you'll see many of his priceless legacies throughout the country. Just a kilometre or two to the south is **Alise-Sainte-Reine** – an old and famous Roman hilltop site. The Alise part of the name comes from Alesia, of Gallic fame; it was in these placid Burgundian hills that Julius Caesar won his renowned seige victory over Vercingétorix, the commander of the Gauls.

From Alise-Sainte-Reine follow the road that runs alongside the tiny River Ozerain, and then, just three or four kilometres later, climb up to **Flavigny-s-Ozerain**. It's a delight – full of medieval treasures: old houses and streets, fortified walls, a 13th century church, a Bénédictine abbey and, if all that is not enough, a splendid site. The countryside hereabouts has been both painted and written about by many famous people over the centuries.

After those four pleasures head west to another , **Semur-en-Auxois**. Like Noyers it is all but an island – the River **Armançon** loops in a circle around the massive

104   Semur-au-Auxois: Pont Joly and the northern start of the Armançon *loop*

walls of the old Burgundian town. Gigantic towers, precipitous views, tree-lined avenues – it's a classic place, the same now as it was centuries ago.

Approximately midway between Semur-en-Auxois and Avallon is **Epoisses**, renowned for its cheese, its ancient town and its fortified château. Avallon is the northern gateway to the **Morvan Regional Park** – it's also on the doorstep of many other priceless Burgundian historical jewels. Explore the town first – its name has Celtic origins, part of ancient British legend. It is full of interesting churches, buildings, streets, ramparts, promenades and viewpoints. Joan of Arc, Napoléon, Mrs Simpson, later to become the Duchess of Windsor – all of them passed through this fine town. For me the best feature of all in Avallon is its dramatic site, high above the **Cousin**, one of the prettiest small rivers in France.

Leave Avallon by descending into the Cousin Valley; then follow the gurgling stream to the west – four kilometres of sheer joy. Desert your car and use your legs to see this exquisite nugget of rural delight at its best – that advice applies throughout the 25 areas described in this book. Then use the D957 to head further west to the most inspiring place I know in France – **Vézelay**

I can find no better words to describe it than those I used in *France à la Carte*. You'll first see it from the D957 – high on its hilltop perch. I suppose it must be a combination of reasons why it is so inspiring: the sheer beauty and size of the great Basilica of Ste-Madeleine; the surrounding terraces with their enormous trees; and the views from the heights over the green Burgundian valleys lying under the hill. The sense of history past pulses strongly through your heart: Saint Bernard preached the Second Crusade here; Richard the Lionheart and Philippe-Auguste, arch-enemies, undertook jointly the Third Crusade from this spot; and Thomas à Becket took refuge here. The church was restored by Viollet-le-Duc.

You will linger long at Vézelay – but when the time comes to tear yourself away you have various options open to you: the first takes you a few kilometres north to the **Grottes d'Arcy** – excellent caves which have water as a feature; the second takes you west to old **Clamecy** – a treasure-trove of ancient houses, streets and riverside views (the **Yonne** Valley is full of other pleasures, both upstream and downstream); and a third option takes you south into the glorious Morvan Regional Park – this is where I would head for.

Dozens of *hidden corners* deserve your attention, some fashioned by Mother Nature and some built by man. Both Nature and man combine at **Pierre-Perthuis**, just south of Vézelay. An attractive, wooded gorge has an old bridge over the River **Cure** that flows through the trees on the valley floor. On your way there stop at **St-Père**, lying under the shadow of Vézelay, but with its own church, supposedly designed by Saint Hugh, one of the architects of Lincoln Cathedral.

Recall as you now drive the quiet lanes, in deserted wooded country, that the superb smoked **Morvan** hams come from this corner of France. Also look out for the local goat's milk cheeses – they'll be called by the names of some of the nearby villages: **Dornecy**, **Lormes** and **Vézelay** are three of them.

Follow the Cure upstream – your first port of call should be the handsome château at **Chastellux**. Enjoy **Quarré-les-Tombes** – but it is the country immediately to the south that will please you more: the narrow forestry tracks that pierce the **Forêt Au Duc**; a natural attraction called the **Rocher de la Pérouse** – fine views to the south beyond the Cure Valley will be your reward; the various lakes – the **Lac des Settons** and the two lakes with dams at their northern ends, the **Barrage de Pannesière-Chaumard** and the **Barrage de Chaumeçon**. Drive the lanes that encircle all these silent stretches of water. North of Les Settons be sure to see the cascade at **Gouloux** – particularly impressive after a spell of wet weather.

Just west of **Montsauche** – near **Le Boulard** – is the most poignant cemetery I know in France. Follow the signs that say *Maquis Bernard* – the track gets rough but don't turn back. Hidden in the trees are the graves of 24 members of the French Resistance and two English airmen. What a price was paid by so many brave people to ensure our freedom today; it's a heart-stirring, inspiring place to remember our debt to the hundreds of thousands of soldiers and civilians who died for us.

Château-Chinon rewards you with extensive panoramic views from Le Calvaire above the town. Continue south, driving deep into the woods and hills of the southern part of the Morvan Regional Park. Just before reaching **St-Léger**, detour to the west, on the one-way-only lane that takes you to the summit of **Mont Beuvray**. If you have time make another *deviation* to the west to **St-Honoré**, a small, attractive spa. Finish your exploration at **Autun**. It was an old Roman town, once called the *sister of Rome* by Julius Caesar; its 800 year old Cathedral of Saint-Lazare is its special treasure. Close by, to the east, is the handsome château at Sully – its setting is particularly attractive.

As I finish this chapter I am conscious that I have omitted many of the other pleasures of the Morvan; give the area more than two days of your time and you'll discover them for yourselves.

One of many splendid old streets in medieval Noyers

MAILLY-LE-CHATEAU   Le Castel
Simple hotel/Quiet/Gardens

This *Relais du Silence* sleeps peacefully under the shadow of a 13th century church.
Be absolutely certain to relish the views from the terrace on the edge of the village.
Below you the **Yonne** makes a huge loop – islands divide it into two. A canal, weir
and bridge – and many trees – all combine to paint a superb picture of river scenery
at its best. Descend and enjoy Mailly Le Bas later.
fpm A–B *meals* C *rooms* 12 B–D *closed* Mid Nov–mid Feb. Wed. (Oct–Mar).
post 89590 Mailly-le-Château. Yonne. *phone* (86) 40.43.06.

MONTSAUCHE   Idéal
Very simple hotel/Quiet/Gardens

To the south of the village and not the prettiest of buildings. Compensating for that
is glorious countryside in all directions. Visit the interesting Maison du Parc at **St-
Brisson** – the headquarters of the Morvan Regional Park, where you'll get leaflets
and maps giving details of walks and drives. Enjoy the local *charcuterie, truite du
pays* and *omelette Morvandelle*.
fpm A–B *meals* NC *rooms* 18 A–C *closed* Nov–Easter.
post 58230 Montsauche. Nièvre. *phone* (86) 84.51.26.

QUARRE-LES-TOMBES   Nord et Poste
Simple hotel

Alongside the church and in the middle of this small Morvan village. Visit the
Maison Vauban at nearby **St-Léger-Vauban** – the birthplace of the military archi-
tect. At the **Rocher de la Pérouse** make the steep climb to the circular observation
table at the summit of the rocks (hand-painted tiles illustrate the extensive view).
Dishes here include *jambon du Morvan* and *terrine aux 3 poissons*.
fpm A–B *meals* C *rooms* 35 B–C *closed* Open all the year.
post 89630 Quarré-les-Tombes. Yonne. *phone* (86) 32.24.55.

SEMUR-EN-AUXOIS   Lac
Comfortable hotel/Quiet/Terrace/GC

Alongside a small lake called the **Lac de Pont** (south of Semur) – its attractions
include bathing facilities. The hotel is a modern building with a shaded terrace.
Specialities include *truite de Fontenay* – you'll see the trout farm where they come
from if you visit the abbey at Fontenay. Other Burgundian treats are *jambon
persillé, escargots* and a range of *local* cheeses and wines.
fpm A–B *meals* NC *rooms* 23 A–D *closed* Mid Dec–end Jan. Sun evg. Mon (except
July–Aug). *post* 21140 Semur-en-Auxois. Côte-d'Or. *phone* (80) 97.11.11.

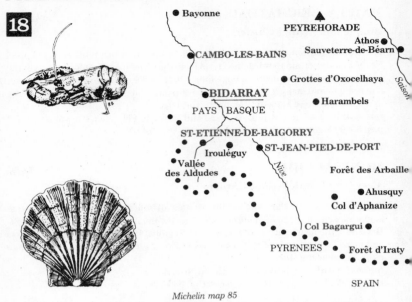

18

Bayonne

PEYREHORADE

Athos
Sauveterre-de-Béarn

CAMBO-LES-BAINS

Grottes d'Oxocelhaya

BIDARRAY

PAYS BASQUE

Harambels

ST-ETIENNE-DE-BAIGORRY

Irouléguy   ST-JEAN-PIED-DE-PORT

Vallée
des Aldudes

Nive

Forêt des Arbaille

Ahusquy
Col d'Aphanize

Col Bagargui

PYRENEES   Forêt d'Iraty

Saison

SPAIN

Michelin map 85

The **Pyrénées** are amongst the most unusual and captivating of European mountain ranges: they link two seas completely different from each other – the Atlantic and the Mediterranean; they separate the two nations of France and Spain. The character of the mountains changes as you travel from the gentler hills in the west to the savage, stark peaks in the centre and then, finally, to the semi-tropical vegetation of the Mediterranean seaboard. I've split the Pyrénées into three areas – try all of them!

My map of this area divides into two separate sections; the **Pays Basque** in the western half and **Béarn** in the east. Let's look first at the Pays Basque; your visit may well include time spent at the many famous resorts and towns that border the Atlantic – Biarritz, St-Jean-de-Luz and **Bayonne** are examples – but I've set myself different terms of reference which will take us to quieter backwaters, some of which see precious few tourists, believe me.

The picturesque and most charmingly-named road – the Route impériale des Cimes – provides the perfect way of leaving Bayonne and heading inland. **Cambo-les-Bains** is the ideal place to start your exploration. It's a mixture of typical Basque village and small spa; as I write these words I can visualise its splendid trees when I saw them last during the month of April; I remember the many green tints of the trees above the River **Nive** and the bright splashes of contrasting colours of camellias and rhododendrons. How just it would be if the wise folk who planted those trees centuries ago could enjoy them now. Edmond Rostand, the author of *Cyrano de Bergerac*, lived at Cambo; his home, the Villa Arnaga, houses the Rostand Museum. To the east of Cambo are the splendid underground caves at the **Grottes**

see page 114

•Orthez

Gave d'Oloron

•Navarrenx

Jurançon• • PAU

•Mauléon-Licharre

BEARN

•OLORON-STE-MARIE

Gave d'Ossau

•Trois-Villes

Lanne• •Aramits

TARDETS-SORHOLUS

Col de Marie-Blanque

Gave d'Aspe

•Ayduis   Col d'Aubisque

Laruns•

Eaux-Bonnes

Lescun•

PARC NATIONAL DES PYRENEES   ▲ Pic du Midi d'Ossau

•Col du Somport•   •Col du Pourtalet

d'Oxocelhaya – the first of many caves in the Pyrénées.

The Nive continues south-east from Cambo-les-Bains; one of its tributaries flows down the **Vallée des Aldudes**. Explore it to your heart's content; I can recall another visit to this part of the world when one hot, spring day, my wife and I savoured the most pleasant of lunches, on a riverside terrace, at the Hôtel Arcé in **St-Etienne-de-Baïgorry**. We lingered long on that sun-trap terrace. After enjoying it all, go past **Irouléguy** – a small amount of excellent local wine comes from the vineyards you'll see on your route – to **St-Jean-Pied-de-Port**.

What a superb town this is – surrounded as it is by lovely country. The Nive provides the perfect complement to the picturesque old houses and, above it, the citadel of the Ville Haute. It was an important stopping-place on the road to Santiago de Compostela in northern Spain and, in the vicinity of this Pyrénées town, are many pilgrimage sites, all clearly marked with the shell sign of Saint Jacques. *Port* means pass – and rising sharply to the south is the climb the pilgrims made to their next objective of Roncevaux in Spain; legend has it that Roland died on the pass. (The most unusual of the sites is at Harambeltz – a 12th century gem – **Harambels** on the map; north-east of St-Jean. Ask at the farm for the key.)

In this area you'll see many examples of the high, unusually-shaped walls used for the Basque game of *pelota* – St-Jean-Pied-de-Port is one of its strongest centres; if you can, see the game in action – it's an exciting spectacle.

Don't fail to leave these lovely corners without trying some of the culinary delights of the region: *pipérade* – an omelette-like mixture of peppers, tomatoes, onions, and sometimes ham; *salmis de palombes* – wood pigeons sautéed in red

109

wine, ham and mushrooms; *gâteau Basque* – a pastry with a baked fruit interior; **Izarra** (this means *star*) is an excellent liqueur with two varieties, yellow and green. The famous *Bayonne* ham, cured and then eaten raw, is another delight – most of them are 'imported' and are cured with *sel de Bayonne* in **Orthez**; indeed, the whole area is renowned for its pork products – its *charcuterie*.

The most appropriate way of leaving the Pays Basque requires you to set aside time, use Michelin map 85 carefully, and head to the south-east of St-Jean-Pied-de-Port. The southernmost route takes you deep into the fine **Forêt d'Iraty** and then climbs high up the **Col Bagargui** – an exciting road requiring great care. An excellent cheese – **Iraty** – comes from these pastures – made from a mixture of cow's and ewe's milk; you'll see some of the farms where it is made. Equally demanding is the climb up the minor road to the **Col d'Aphanize** and on to **Ahusquy**; this skirts the southern edges of the **Forêt des Arbailles**. Either route brings you eventually into the **Saison** Valley. It's splendid, thrilling terrain.

Now you are in Béarn country. **Mauléon-Licharre** is an old fortified stronghold. Aramis of *The Three Musketeers* took his name from **Aramits**; **Lanne**, just west of Aramits, was the home of Monsieur de Porthau – who gave his name to Porthos; and the hamlet called **Trois-Villes**, 11 kilometres south of Mauléon, gave its name to Tréville. All those place names are clearly shown on the Michelin map; **Athos** is just west of **Sauveterre-de-Béarn**.

The River Saison flows north and joins the more important **Gave d'Oloron** near Sauveterre-de-Béarn. The latter is a splendid place, picturesquely situated alongside the river; the riverside views and the 12th century bridge, so important to

St-Jean-Pied-de-Port: reflections in the Nive

those pilgrims heading south, are its special attractions.

The Gave d'Oloron is a renowned salmon river; downstream from Sauveterre-de-Béarn it is at its best in February and March; April and May see the next stretch southwards to **Navarrenx** at its best; the 40 kilometres upstream from the latter to **Oloron-Ste-Marie** are at their peak in June, July and August. Under no circumstances should you miss the chance to enjoy these locally-caught salmon; equally, you must not ignore the local **Béarn** wines and the renowned ones from **Jurançon**, south of **Pau**. From the latter you'll enjoy both sweet and dry (*sec*) whites; the sweet variety (*moelleux*) is the perfect complement to *foie gras*.

Navarrenx, a medieval fortified town, played an important part in the defence of this river country and it, too, lay on one of the pilgrims' routes to St-Jean-Pied-de-Port. So did Oloron-Ste-Marie, further upstream; it's a handsome town with a fine setting at the point the Gave d'Oloron splits into two – the **Gave d'Aspe** and the Gave d'Ossau. The Eglise Ste-Marie, built in the 13th century, has a fascinating portal which you should certainly seek out.

The Aspe and the Ossau are also renowned for their fishing; not salmon in this case, but trout and char – the Aspe is particularly highly thought of. Fisherman or not, both valleys deserve some of your time. Several *dead-end* roads climb up into the hills that line the Vallée d'Aspe: to the east is the short run to **Ayduis**; to the west is the pretty setting of the hills circling **Lescun** – particularly pleasant views are to be had from the slopes above the village. The *Col du Somport* marks the point where the Spanish border lies; at the summit you will have entered for the first time the **Parc National des Pyrénées** which skirts the border eastwards. Marvellous views reward you from the col – as you enjoy them, recall that this crossing point was important even in the days of the Romans.

To reach the Vallée d'Ossau from this point, you must retrace your steps and use the **Col de Marie-Blanque** to head eastwards. It's another classic example where it pays to climb as high as you can – in this case either to the head of the valley at the **Col du Pourtalet** or, better still, up the four kilometres *dead-end* lane to the lake below the **Pic du Midi d'Ossau**. **Eaux-Bonnes** has an attractive site and is the gateway to the *Central Pyrénées*, via the high **Col d'Aubisque**. Try the local ewe's milk cheese called **Laruns**, made in the Ossau Valley. It's also renowned for its marvellous wild flowers.

We finish our tour by driving north to Pau but, on the way, consider some of the specialities of Béarn which you must try to enjoy during your travels: *tourin* or *ouillat* – onion soup with garlic: *cousinette* or *cousinat* – vegetable soup, made with leeks, carrots and beans; *garbure* – the most famous of all vegetable soups, often made with cabbage or pork or *confit* of goose and served in two parts – the broth, followed by the main ingredients of the soup; finally, *poule au pot* – the chicken dish that was given its name by the legendary Henri IV of Navarre who became one of France's greatest kings.

Pau is where Henri was born. The château in this lovely town, with its exquisite grace and Edwardian elegance, is full of reminders of his birth and early days. But the town is endowed with many other charms; amongst them the classic Boulevard des Pyrénées – with its view of the majestic mountains to the south – and its pretty parks. It makes the ideal place to finish your touring of the area.

112   Oloron-Ste-Marie: the glorious Romanesque west door at the Eglise Ste-Marie

BIDARRAY
Pont d'Enfer

Comfortable hotel/Quiet/Terrace/Gardens

The standard red and white livery of the area for this *Logis de France*, on the west bank of the Nive, away from the main road. There is a terrace by the riverside to complement the pleasure of trying the local Basque specialities which include: *poulet Basquaise, pipérade au jambon, jambon Bayonne* and *gâteau Basque*; trout are also prepared in several different ways.

fpm A *meals* C *rooms* 18 A–D *closed* Nov–Feb.

post Bidarray. 64780 Osses. Pyr.-Atl. *phone* (59) 37.09.67.

OLORON-STE-MARIE
Béarn

Comfortable hotel/Lift

Years ago this hotel had a Michelin star; it's in a relatively quiet spot alongside the *Mairie*, but away from the busy main road through this bustling, nice town. Enjoy salmon from the local rivers, many local cheeses, *salmis de palombe, magret de canard* and the really fine wines from the hills at **Jurançon**, near **Pau**. Don't miss the Eglise Ste-Marie with its splendid portal.

fpm B–D *meals* NC *rooms* 32 B–E *closed* Feb. Sat and Sun (out of season).

post 4 Pl.Mairie. 64400 Oloron-Ste-Marie. Pyr.-Atl. *phone* (59) 39.00.99.

TARDETS-SORHOLUS
Gave

Simple hotel/Gardens

The hotel overlooks a river and has what can only be described as the most basic of gardens (a general **caveat** – don't expect to find the English equivalent in French gardens). Dinners only at this establishment with dishes like *œuf pipérade*, *omelette Basquaise* and *profiteroles*. To the north and east is gentle, rolling hill country, full of reminders of *The Three Musketeers*.

fpm A–B *meals* NC *rooms* 14 B–D *closed* Nov–Feb. Mon.

post 64470 Tardets-Sorholus. Pyr.-Atl. *phone* (59) 28.53.67.

TARDETS-SORHOLUS
Pont d'Abense

Simple restaurant with rooms/Quiet/Terrace/Gardens

Another white building with red shutters; it's a near neighbour of the Gave but across the river in a nicer site – the terrace is particularly inviting. Good-value menus with dishes like *truite meunière, asperges vinaigrette* and *gâteau Basque*. Don't miss the exciting run south via the **Col Bagargui** to **St-Jean-Pied-de-Port**; much of it is reminiscent of scenery in Wales.

fpm A–B *meals* C *rooms* 12 A–C *closed* Mid Nov–Dec. Fri (out of season).

post Abense de Haut. 64470 Tardets-Sorholus. Pyr.-Atl. *phone* (59) 28.54.60.

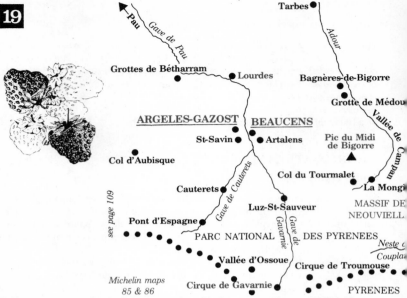

19

If, like me, you are hooked on mountains, this is an area where you'll be in your element – all of it is high mountain country with just a handful of valleys running like open fingers of a hand, southwards towards the high barrier of the Franco/Spanish border. The peaks making up that barrier rise to a maximum height of between 3000 and 3500 metres; that is not high when compared with the Alps, but, when you see them from the northern approaches, you are at a relatively modest height above sea-level. Consequently the whole range has a wild, massive grandeur about it – the peaks rise higher and higher as you travel south.

I think the area is at its best in April and May; unhappily, at that time of year, many of the high passes which straddle the peaks in an east-west direction are closed. If you want to revel in the splendour of those solitary peaks then your journey must be in the summer months. Nature will be your host hereabouts – though there are some interesting man-made attractions to compete with her in the dazzling show that awaits you.

Let's assume we approach the area from **Pau** (where the *Western Pyrénées* chapter finished). Follow the banks of the **Gave de Pau** (*gave* means river); your first halt will be at the **Grottes de Bétharram**. These are magnificent limestone caves where water is a feature: a *télécabine*, punts, and a small train all combine to move you about this dramatic curiosity; don't miss it. Further upstream you'll get your first, and best, view of **Lourdes**. The events that have taken place there in the years since 1858, when Bernadette Soubirous first saw the Virgin Mary in a cave alongside the southern bank of the Gave de Pau, are known by all; suffice it to say that a visit at anytime is always memorable, particularly if it includes participating

114

see page 120

in one of the outdoor processions and services.

South of Lourdes are a whole series of sights. **Argelès-Gazost** is a spa town; two detours are essential in the hills to the immediate south. The first is to the Romanesque abbey at **St-Savin**; the second is the pretty and steep climb to **Artalens** across the valley from St-Savin. If you approach the mountains from the west, Argelès-Gazost is at the eastern end of the first really high pass in the **Pyrénées**, the **Col d'Aubisque**. It's a tortuous climb; take care and remember, as you climb and descend, the annual Tour de France and those brave cyclists who are put on the rack each summer in these mountains.

Just below St-Savin you can ascend the first of many super *dead-end* valleys in this section of the Pyrénées – the **Gave de Cauterets**. **Cauterets** is another spa that was known in Roman times; its site is more attractive than most. It's famous, too, for its *berlingots* – burnt-sugar, fruity-tasting sweets. Continue up towards **Pont d'Espagne**. There's a series of splendid waterfalls, at their best in late spring. As I say many times within the pages of this book, make *dead-end* roads one of your main objectives as you explore each area; this example proves yet again that the best scenery is often seen from them. On the drive you will enter for the first time the magnificent **Parc National des Pyrénées**; you'll relish more of it later as you head eastwards.

An alternative route from St-Savin takes you past **Luz-St-Sauveur** up the **Gave de Gavarnie** – don't miss the ancient fortified church at Luz. About 10 kilometres from Luz the road splits into two; both take you up *dead-ends* to two of the most dramatic sites in France. The more famous of the two is the mighty **Cirque de**

Gavarnie – *cirque* means *amphitheatre* of mountains. The Gavarnie *cirque* has vertical rock faces – rising in several stages, and each stage as much as 500 metres high – surrounding you on three sides. In late spring dozens of waterfalls cascade down the rock faces. Its other neighbour, to the east, is the **Cirque de Troumouse** – not as spectacular but yet another formidable wall of mountains stops you in your tracks. Don't leave the village of Gavarnie without making the two steep climbs up to the Port de Gavarnie and the far from easy ascent up the **Vallée d'Ossoue**. In early May – south of Luz – I thrilled at the sight of pastures full of wild daffodils.

The **Adour** Valley runs south from **Tarbes** and is another of the important fingers that run south to north. **Bagnères-de-Bigorre** is its major town – an extremely busy spa. On its southern flanks is the **Grotte de Médous** where, once more, water plays a part in creating interest for visitors. The caves are illuminated and your visit will include the use of a punt. As you continue south the valley becomes known as the **Vallée de Campan**; it loops to the south-west and a mighty pass, the **Col du Tourmalet**, links it with the town of Luz.

The valley of the Campan has been described by many as the most beautiful in the Pyrénées; perhaps so – I leave you to judge for yourself. What I do know is that it repays any efforts made to drive up it. The Tourmalet is an exciting climb – at the top of the col a toll road takes you close to the 2865 metres high summit called **Pic du Midi de Bigorre**, where there's a TV transmitter, an observatory and one of the most staggering views in the entire Pyrénées. An alternative way of getting to the summit is by using the *téléphérique* from **La Mongie**.

You can pass from the Campan Valley to the next of the fingers – the **Vallée**

Cirque de Gavarnie: seek it out and its neighbour – the Cirque de Troumouse

The superb Massif de Néouvielle viewed from the Col d'Aspin

d'Aure – by making use of the best of all the high passes in the Pyrénées, the **Col d'Aspin**. It is nothing like as high as the others but its particular charms are the lovely forests on its western flanks and the vast panoramic views from the col itself. The valley floor to the east serves as one of the main roads that cross into Spain; use it to a point just nine kilometres west of **St-Lary-Soulan** and then turn north up yet one more *dead-end* road, climbing up alongside the charmingly-named torrent, the **Neste de Couplan**. Waterfalls, woods and finally man-made lakes will be your reward; with the added bonus of peace and quiet. At the point the road finishes you are on the flanks of the majestic **Massif de Néouvielle**. Another track runs south from St-Lary-Soulan up the even more deserted and wooded **Vallée du Rioumajou** – several waterfalls add extra interest here.

The **Col de Peyresourde** carries you over its 1569 metres high summit and down to **Bagnères-de-Luchon**. On the descent, if time allows, visit at least one of the three old churches in the villages of **St-Pé**, **Cazeaux** and **St-Aventin**. The spa town of Luchon (its abbreviated, more common name), is another busy, flourishing place. Southwards from the spa are two glorious *dead-end* valleys: the western fork is the **Vallée du Lys**; the other is called the **Vallée de la Pique** and climbs up to the Hospice de France. Both are endowed with delightful wooded slopes and roaring torrents and there's many a cascade; try to see them both. The Vallée du Lys also provides the access road that snakes northwards to the winter-sports resort of **Superbagnères**, another of the killing Tour de France special stages.

The **Vallée d'Oueil** runs north-west from Luchon and the road that follows its northern slopes eventually peters out at a height of some 1855 metres; needless to say the views are renowned. 18 kilometres north of Luchon you'll see the River **Garonne** for the first time as it flows on its long journey towards the Atlantic. The wooded hills that border its banks hide some charming villages and small hotels; the **Col de Portet-d'Aspet** gives easy access to the *Eastern Pyrénées*. But before you desert this pretty corner of countryside, there remain two sights you must visit, both away from main roads.

The first is the medieval walled village of **St-Bertrand-de-Comminges** with its amazing *cathédrale*. This building is part Romanesque, part Gothic – its treasure is the 16th century choir stalls. In Roman times this small place was part of a town that boasted a population of 50,000 souls; Herod was exiled here by Caligula. Nearby are some prehistoric caves – the **Grottes de Gargas**.

Finally, a piece of advice that, though given here, also applies to any part of France. Sunday is the ideal day to enjoy either a picnic or a visit to a restaurant for lunch. On one Sunday of your holiday relish the sight of a *pâtisserie* – full of mouth-watering confections baked for local clients; you'll need some francs in your pocket as you'll not be able to resist the temptation to share in those treats. The *charcu-terie*, too, is seen at its best in shops on a Sunday, not just pork products in endless varieties, but a wide selection of cooked vegetables and other delights, too, are usually on show.

You'll have to use another Sunday to have a midday lunch; book ahead if you are going to join the endless number of French families – from grandparents down to the newest babe in arms – thronging around the restaurant tables. It's a tradition that really does help to keep French families together.

The *cathédrale* at St-Bertrand-de-Comminges

ANTICHAN Host. Ourse
Simple hotel/Quiet/Gardens

A prettily-sited, white building with red shutters. It's alongside the River Ourse and is well placed for you to explore all the mountains to the immediate south; nearby is the *cathédrale* at **St-Bertrand-de-Comminges** (don't miss it) and the Basilique St-Just de Valcabrère. Dishes are basic – trout and cheeses are both local and good. Dinner served to residents only.
fpm A–B *meals* NC *rooms* 10 A–C *closed* Sept. Nov–Easter. Fri (out of season).
post Antichan. 65370 Loures-Barousse. H.-Pyr. *phone* (62) 99.25.02.

ARGELES-GAZOST Miramont
Comfortable hotel/Terrace/Gardens

An extremely smart, unusually-shaped, modern hotel. It is close to a pleasant, circular park and it has open views south towards the **Pyrénées**. Classical cuisine of a fairly high standard. Menus include: *saumon frais au beurre blanc, steak au poivre, jambon du pays, salade Niçoise* and other tasty alternatives. **Fromage des Pyrénées** is also well worth trying.
fpm A–B *meals* C *rooms* 29 B–C *closed* Mid Oct–mid Dec. Rest only: Mon (mid Jan–Apl).
post Rue Pasteur. 65400 Argelès-Gazost. H.-Pyr. *phone* (62) 97.01.26.

BEAUCENS Thermal
Simple hotel/Secluded/Terrace/Gardens

What a delightful spot; the hotel is in fact the thermal resort of Beaucens (the spring is under the building). The cooking is truly modest but the compensation for that is a large, green park, utter seclusion and the ability to head southwards and be thrilled by the magnificent *cirques* at **Gavarnie** and **Troumouse**. Alternatively, stay put on the terrace, put your legs up and enjoy life!
fpm A–B *meals* NC *rooms* 28 B–D *closed* Oct–mid May.
post Beaucens. 65400 Argelès-Gazost. H.-Pyr. *phone* (62) 97.04.21.

ENCAUSSE-LES-THERMES Marronniers
Comfortable rest. with rooms (no baths or showers)/Quiet/Terrace

Another white building with the statutory red shutters – this one, too, is alongside a river. Here you have the bonus of a shaded terrace between the building and the stream. The establishment has a longstanding reputation for good cuisine. A variety of local products appear on the menus: *jambon, pâtés, saucisson, cèpes* and *jambonneau*; try the dessert called *gateau des prélats.*
fpm A–B *meals* C *rooms* 12 A *closed* Oct. Mon (Nov–Feb).
post Encausse-les-Thermes. 31160 Aspet. H.-Gar. *phone* (61) 89.17.12.

Grotte du Mas-d'Azil ●

● St-Lizier   ● Labouiche
● ST-GIRONS   ● Foix

Col de Péguère ● ● Col de Jouels   ● Roquefixade
● Vallée de Bethmale   Col de Port
Oust ●   **MASSAT** ●   Tarascon-sur-Ariège

● Vallée du Garbet   ● Grotte de Niaux

Vallée d'Ustou ●   ● Aulus-les-Bains   **UNAC**

● Col de Pause   Ax-les-Thermes ●

see page 115

PYRENEES

SPAIN

Ariège

ANDORRA

Michelin maps 83 & 86

In my opinion much the very best way of entering this magnificent mass of country is through the gateway in the north-east corner – the town of Carcassonne. I asked this same question in *France à la Carte*: is there a more romantic skyline anywhere else in France? It is a massive, impressive fortress – the largest in Europe. You'll walk the narrow streets within the awesome walls of *La Cité* absorbing its many splendours – but it is no coincidence that the best views of this, the finest of fortified towns, are from the banks of the River **Aude**, to the south of Carcassonne. Be certain, too, to gasp at the same sight at night – a floodlighting spectacle par excellence. I suggest that after you have enjoyed those views, leave Carcassonne behind you and follow the Aude Valley, climbing steadily higher as you travel south to within a few kilometres of its source.

The first town you reach is **Limoux** – it's not very significant for any special scenic reasons, but it is certainly renowned for its splendid, inexpensive, sparkling white wine called **Blanquette de Limoux**; it's claimed to be the oldest *sparkler* in the world and its name came from the original name of the vine – so called because of the fine white down that covers the underside of its leaves. Just as you would have undoubtedly tried the famous *cassoulet* of Carcassonne and Castelnaudary (based on white kidney beans, pork and goose), so you must savour this lovely white wine. The soft and fruity red wines of **Corbières** – from the hills to the east of Limoux – would perhaps be the more appropriate wines to accompany many of the rather heavy local recipes of Languedoc; though the sparkling wines of Limoux go well with *cassoulet* – in my opinion an overrated, indigestible dish.

Further down the valley, at **Couiza**, make the short, sharp climb to **Rennes-le-**

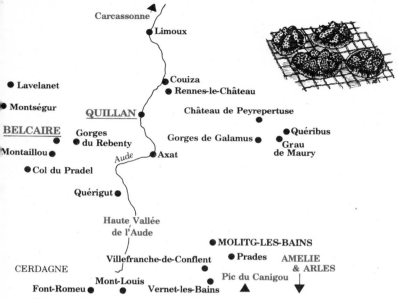

Carcassonne

Limoux

Lavelanet

Montségur

Couiza
Rennes-le-Château

QUILLAN

Château de Peyrepertuse

BELCAIRE

Gorges
du Rebenty

Gorges de Galamus

Quéribus
Grau
de Maury

Montaillou

Aude

Axat

Col du Pradel

Quérigut

Haute Vallée
de l'Aude

MOLITG-LES-BAINS

Prades

Villefranche-de-Conflent

AMELIE
& ARLES

CERDAGNE

Mont-Louis

Pic du Canigou

Font-Romeu

Vernet-les-Bains

Château. There's a vast, panoramic view; you'll have an added reason for making this four kilometres detour if you have read the controversial, bestselling book called *The Holy Blood and the Holy Grail* (publishers – Cape), as the events that took place in this remote spot played a vital part in the claims made in the book.

Like Limoux, there is nothing special about **Quillan**, the next small town on your travels south, but 12 kilometres later, at **Axat**, the scenery becomes quite sensational. Here you enter the **Haute Vallée de l'Aude** – a wonderland of visual intoxication. The next 57 kilometres are a mixture of pleasures – high mountains, glorious forests and spectacular gorges all unite to put on an impressive show. I've seen it at various times of the year – but in April, when the torrent is in flood with clear, pure water, and the newly-opened buds of green abound everywhere – then it is at its best. Just before you reach the first of two lakes near the river's source, double back to the north to **Quérigut**; its ruined castle was built by the Cathars over 700 years ago – it is one of many in the area.

Your final destination is the high plateau where you'll find two towns: **Mont-Louis** is an old walled place with fortifications designed by Vauban; **Font-Romeu** (its name means *The Pilgrim's Fountain*) is a new, modern resort, spread amongst the pines – it's regularly used by athletes for altitude training. All this is part of the **Cerdagne** – the name given to this high, verdant plateau.

If your interests are not of the scenic sort, an alternative route would take you east from Limoux through Corbières country to a truly magnificent structure – partly ruined now – the **Château de Peyrepertuse**. Nature competes nearby with two of her own attractions – the **Gorges de Galamus**; and the **Grau de Maury**, a small pass with fine views. One kilometre from the pass is another of the many ruined, 700 year old Cathar strongholds found in the eastern Pyrénées – the splendid castle at **Quéribus**. Make the effort to seek it out.

From there you could navigate yourself along the twisting, narrow roads that climb up and down, eventually reaching **Prades**; but, before you make the final four kilometres descent into the town, detour up into the hills to **Molitg-les-Bains**, a green oasis in the dry hills. Prades is known throughout the world by music lovers for its Music Festival, founded by the cellist Pablo Casals; it takes place at the nearby Monastery of St-Michel-de-Cuxa. Climb past it and descend to the sheltered and green spa of **Vernet-les-Bains**, lying in the shadow of the massive Pic du Canigou. If you are really energetic make the long steep walk up to the small and perfectly proportioned 10th century abbey at St-Martin-du-Canigou, *perched* high above Vernet-les-Bains. Explore the covered ramparts of nearby medieval **Villefranche-de-Conflent**. You can finish this long run by driving west up into the high Cerdagne, rejoining the previous route.

An alternative way of seeing something of the Cerdagne is to use the exciting, open-air *La Voie Metrique* train – called the *Canari* because of its red and yellow livery; it climbs from Villefranche-de-Conflent (alt. 427 metres) to its highest point in the Cerdagne of 1592 metres.

The River **Ariège** cuts the area shown on the accompanying map in two. It's possible you have travelled south from Toulouse – if so, the first place of interest you reach is **Foix**; towering above the town are the three different shaped towers of its castle. There is a great deal of splendid country to the west, but first seek out the

The modern-day Montaillou: read the book before you visit the tiny village

many attractions that lie to the east.

The first two sites are further examples of the many castles – all now in ruins – built in these hills over seven centuries ago: **Roquefixade** comes shortly before you reach **Lavelanet** on the D9; the more famous one, **Montségur**, is south of Lavelanet and lost in the hills. Montségur was the last Cathar fortress to fall. (Cathars were also known as Albigensians, taking their name from the town of Albi; see the chapter called *Haut Languedoc*.) The siege of Montségur lasted six months – at the end of it, in 1244, 200 Cathars were burnt at the stake.

By the beginning of the 14th century the Albigensian heresy had revived in a small way – its main centre was the village of **Montaillou**. You'll locate it just a few kilometres south-east of Montségur and west of Belcaire. I strongly recommend you to buy the book called *Montaillou* (published by Penguin) – it tells the story of the Cathars in this high, remote and minute mountain village during the period 1294–1324. It is compulsive reading; I know of no more dramatic way of bringing medieval history and present-day geography together. Seek the modern-day village out *after* you have read the book – you'll be fascinated by it.

Leave Montaillou and head east, via the narrow D20, to the splendid **Gorges du Rebenty**. Then head south and climb the high **Col du Pradel** – it is a difficult road but the views from the pass are glorious and make the effort worthwhile.

Descend to **Ax-les-Thermes**, a small spa town. At this point you may choose to see the so-called delights of **Andorra**; but that alternative is not for me, and as far as I can recall, has pleased few of my friends. Instead head back towards Foix, but, just before **Tarascon-sur-Ariège**, detour south-west to the **Grotte de Niaux** with its prehistoric wall paintings.

To the north-west of Foix are two exciting underground attractions: the first, and closest to the town, is the underground cave at **Labouiche** – the main feature is a subterranean river and you can explore some kilometres of it by boat; the second is the dry, illuminated cave called **Grotte du Mas-d'Azil** – renowned for its specimens of prehistoric paintings of bison on the cave walls.

If, like me, you really prefer the open-air delights of mountain country, you'll head west and south-west from Foix. None of these green, wooded hills rise to great heights – all you'll see of the high **Pyrénées** are the peaks lining the border between Spain and France to the south. You can make a start to enjoy the hills by using the easy climb up the **Col de Port**. As an alternative you can use the somewhat harder Route Verte, the D17, that climbs due west of Foix up to the **Col de Jouels**. Whichever route you choose your objective should be the **Col de Péguère** – the views are superb. Descend to the mountain village of **Massat**.

Nearby **Oust** is the starting point for a drive that takes you first up the **Vallée du Garbet** to the small spa of **Aulus-les-Bains**, and then, westwards, down the **Vallée d'Ustou** towards Oust. Five kilometres before Oust, make a *deviation* south to the *dead-end* **Col de Pause**. Some of the best countryside is to be found up roads that go nowhere; this 1527 metres high climb proves that conclusively. From Oust make a final mountain loop, via the truly delightful **Vallée de Bethmale**, to **St-Girons**. There's nothing special about St-Girons, but you mustn't miss nearby **St-Lizier**; the Cathedral of St-Lizier dates from the 11th century, has fine frescoes in its interior and particularly impressive two-tier cloisters.

123

124　　Two tiers of cloisters at the cathedral in St-Lizier

BELCAIRE   Bayle

Very simple hotel

A modest *Logis de France*; but both the Kléber and Michelin guides give it credit for good cooking. (Kléber, sadly, have now stopped publishing their guide.) Don't under any circumstances miss the **Gorges du Rebenty**, the forests to the immediate north-west of the village, and, of course, seek out the modern-day **Montaillou** (read the Penguin paperback, *Montaillou*, first).
fpm A–C *meals* C *rooms* 16 A–B *closed* Oct. Rest only: Fri evg and Sat midday (out of season). *post* Belcaire. 11340 Espezel. Aude. *phone* (68) 20.31.05.

MASSAT   Trois Seigneurs

Comfortable hotel/Quiet/Terrace/Gardens

For decades this hotel has had a sound reputation for a high standard of cuisine. Certainly some innovative and interesting touches appear on the menus: *mousse de foie gras* and *saucisson de marcassin* are examples. The building is a large, chalet-style place on the **St-Girons** road. One drive you must not miss is the lovely **Vallée de Bethmale** run (south of St-Girons and west of Massat).
fpm A–C *meals* NC *rooms* 25 B–C *closed* Nov–Feb.
post 09320 Massat. Ariège. *phone* (61) 96.95.89.

QUILLAN   Cartier

Comfortable hotel

A modern, smart place – with extensions nearly completed to add extra bedrooms and facilities. A local soup – *rouzolle* – makes a change from the inevitable *cassoulet*. Perfect for exploring Cathar country: the ruined fortresses of **Montségur** to the west, **Quérigut** to the south and **Quéribus** to the east should be part of your itinerary. Don't bypass the superb **Haute Vallée de l'Aude**.
fpm A–C *meals* NC *rooms* 28 A–D *closed* Mid Dec–mid Mar.
post Bd. Ch.-de-Gaulle. 11500 Quillan. Aude. *phone* (68) 20.05.14.

UNAC   L'Oustal

Comfortable rest. with rooms (no baths or showers)Secluded/GC

A tiny place, perched high above the River **Ariège** in the hamlet of Unac – nine kilometres north-west of **Ax-les-Thermes**. It's clearly very popular with locals and no wonder. Menus include the following specialities: *truite grillée au feu de bois beurre blanc, écrevisses à ma façon, soupe de poisson maison, foie de canard* and *matelote anguille* – and these are just a few of them.
fpm B–D *meals* C *rooms* 8 A–B *closed* Jan. Tues and Wed (mid Sept–mid June).
post Unac. 09250 Luzenac. Ariège. *phone* (61) 64.48.44.

LA SUISSE NORMANDE

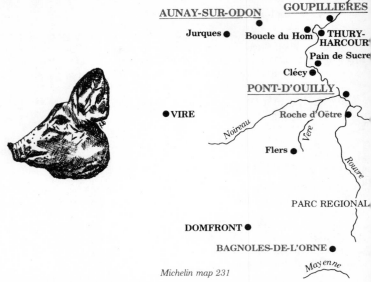

Clinchamps-s-Orne

GOUPILLIÈRES

AUNAY-SUR-ODON

Jurques Boucle du Hom THURY-HARCOUR'

Pain de Sucre

Clécy

PONT-D'OUILLY

VIRE Roche d'Oëtre

Noireau

Vère

Flers

Rouvre

PARC REGIONAL

DOMFRONT

BAGNOLES-DE-L'ORNE

Mayenne

Michelin map 231

I am using the term *La Suisse Normande* to describe an area which, strictly speaking, covers countryside extending beyond the correct geographical definition commonly applied to it. This delightful description – often called in English *little Switzerland* – is given to just a small part of Normandy: it's right in the centre of my map and is a small circle of wooded hills and river gorges. Don't in any sense think of it as the more normal and popular image of Switzerland – it resembles more closely the Jura hills. You will notice my map extends from the suburbs of Caen in the north to the magnificent forests of the **Parc Régional Normandie-Maine** in the south; and from **Vire** in the west to the River **Touques** in the east.

It's all intoxicating country – in more senses than one. In May, it is an especially delicious place; the fields are full of wild yellow irises and great apple orchards are laden down with blossom destined to become that strong and fiery apple brandy, **Calvados**. It is full of dazzling brown and white timbered cottages, many of them beautifully restored. I imagine that this area, more than any other of the 25 I have chosen to describe to you, is seen by a great number of people; nevertheless, thousands pass it by on their hectic drives to and from Channel ports – completely ignoring its many, many charms.

Let's begin by concentrating on those charms that please the tastebuds. Start your tasting in the Touques Valley in the north-east corner. The emerald pastures that abound there are Mother Nature's food powerhouse; a land of cattle, and consequently, milk and cheese. The terrain is more commonly known as the Auge Region or the **Vallée d'Auge**: world-famous cheeses are made at **Livarot** – a semi-hard, strong gold variety; at **Pont-l'Evêque** (just north of **Lisieux**) – a soft gold

126

Caen

Lisieux
St-Germain-de-Livet
St-Pierre-s-Dives
Livarot
Vallée d'Auge
Brèche au Diable
Falaise
Camembert
Dives
Orne
Touques
Ménil-Glaise
Argentan
PUTANGES-
PONT-ECREPIN
Haras du Pin
L'AIGLE →
NORMANDIE-MAINE
Château d'O
La Croix de Médavy
Sées
Carrouges
Forêt d'Ecouves
PRE-EN-PAIL

cheese but square shaped; and the most renowned of all – the cheese called
Camembert. It took its name from a village in the valley; the soft, milky-flavour
cheese, produced as a small, flat disk, was made famous by Madame Harel at the
end of the 18th century – the small, wooden box in which the cheese is packed was
invented by a Monsieur Ridel in 1890.

Vallée d'Auge gives its name to many Normandy dishes, particularly to chicken,
fish and veal specialities. It always means the addition of cream, apples or cider, or
apple brandy (Calvados), in some form or another; that rich, filling cream of
Normandy is used with great zeal – too much so in my opinion.

The vast harvests of apples are put to good use in many ways. Cider appears
everywhere. Calvados is a *digestive* – distilled apple brandy; there are no less than
10 classified Calvados regions but the best comes from the Vallée d'Auge. The fruit
is also used to make the best apple tart in the world – a *tarte aux pommes chaude*;
cooked by an expert, with fresh cream as an accompaniment, it is a delectable
sweet. *Douillons de pommes à la Normande* are apples wrapped in pastry and
baked (there are pear varieties of this dessert, too).

If all that is not enough, you must also remember that Normandy is one of the
natural homes of the pig – no wonder, as all the wants of that animal are provided by
the orchards and farms. You'll see pork products of all sorts: tripe, black puddings,
pâtès, hams and brawn; but much the most famous are the *andouilles* – smoked
sausages, eaten cold; and *andouillettes* – chitterling sausages, always grilled. The
best come from the town of Vire. This town is also famous for its splendid butter –
both salted and sweet. To cap all this, recall that the sea is just kilometres away,

both to the north and west; so fish appears as a matter of course on many menus – you'll see endless varieties, but particularly good are turbot, halibut and the magnificent Dover sole.

Now what remains to feast the eyes on? A great deal I assure you. After tasting the various treats of the Touques Valley and viewing the unusual moated château at **St-Germain-de-Livet**, head west, through **St-Pierre-s-Dives**, with its abbey church and covered market, to the River **Orne**. You can't do better than soak up the exhilarating atmosphere of the Orne Valley – from a point some 14 kilometres north of **Thury-Harcourt**, at **Clinchamps-s-Orne**. Use the lanes on the western bank; be certain to make the short *deviation* to the **Boucle du Hom** – where the river makes a famous and unusual loop.

To the west of Thury-Harcourt are several fine viewpoints from the first long ridge of hills that are the northern barrier to La Suisse Normande. **Aunay-sur-Odon** took a horrific battering in June 1944 – see its new town; children will enjoy a zoo park at **Jurques**, to the west of Aunay.

Children, too, will get great fun from the lanes and fields that follow the highly scenic and attractive Orne, upstream from Thury-Harcourt. Years ago our children spent happy hours in the fields alongside the river banks. It was a vivid reminder that children are not always exclusively entertained by beaches and the sea. They made friends with a local farmer who allowed them to help with several tasks on his farm, including milking the cows. Those few days spent in the wooded river country left us with happy memories.

Adults will love the river views near **Clécy** – the tourist centre of the area. It's vital

The Orne at Putanges-Pont-Ecrepin: the Lion Verd is to the left

you use the lanes that are in the hills above the east bank of the river – the Michelin map shows the best viewpoint of all, called the **Pain de Sucre**, just north of Clécy. Lose yourself in the wooded hills to the east of the river as you head towards **Pont d'Ouilly**; walking is no hardship hereabouts.

Children and adults alike will want to make a detour to **Falaise** – William the Conqueror was born at the castle there. One entertaining way of hearing the story of William is by attending a *son et lumière* (sound and light) performance; you will hear how Robert (William's father), just 17, fell in love with Arlette, the farmer's daughter, who was even younger. It is said he first saw her from a window in the castle, washing clothes in a pool below the walls – probably so, as the medieval wash houses are still there. What is a fact of course, is that William was born a bastard. The castle suffered terribly during the Second World War as the Germans retreated in August 1944; it has long since been restored. Before returning to the Orne, head north from Falaise for nine kilometres to the unusual gorge called the **Brèche au Diable** (Devil's Breach).

If time allows follow the tiny streams called the **Noireau** and **Vère** – to the west of Pont-d'Ouilly. But is to the south of Pont-d'Ouilly where you'll find the best of all these rocky, wooded hills. There's many a viewpoint – the most exciting is called the **Roche d'Oëtre**, which overlooks the **Rouvre**, a tributary of the Orne. A strange-looking barrage dams the Orne west of **Putanges-Pont-Ecrepin**, with the inevitable man-made lake backing it up. Beyond Putanges, make the effort required to seek out the river views near Ménil-Jean and **Ménil-Glaise**.

To finish off your exploration of this short but delightful river valley, take in the remaining man-made treasures to the south-east of Argentan: the handsome Renaissance and moated **Château d'O**; the cathedral town of **Sées**; and, a special treat for children, **Haras du Pin** – the site of the Le Pin Stud, where 100 or so magnificent stallions are stabled; all of it set in a wooded park and with a splendid château as an added attraction.

You are perfectly placed now to explore what remains of this hidden area – the great forests of the Parc Régional Normandie-Maine. Start in the **Forêt d'Ecouves** – one of the great French forests – full of beeches, oaks, pines and spruce trees. Its highest point is 417 metres above sea-level. Throughout your travels in Normandy you will come across many memorials to the days when the Allies, following the D-Day Landings in June 1944, started their immense push across Europe. You'll see evidence of the terrible destruction everywhere in the shape of new buildings. In the Ecouves forest are monuments of the part the French played in those days of liberation; one of them is a tank at **La Croix de Médavy**.

Continue west via the vast château at **Carrouges** with its elegant interior furnishings, to the attractive spa called **Bagnoles-de-l'Orne** – one of the most immaculate, small towns in France. The small lake, many pretty parks and surrounding woods are a treat. Explore both Bagnoles and nearby Tessé-la-Madeleine (to the south-west) and the Vée Valley between them.

More thick forests line the road that heads west to **Domfront** – but detour south down any one of the side roads and, within a kilometre or two, enjoy the extensive views across the **Mayenne** Valley. Domfront has an impressive site – don't miss the extensive panoramas from its ruined keep above the town.

The Orne at Clécy: at its best in early spring

AUNAY-SUR-ODON   St-Michel
Comfortable rest. with rooms (no showers or baths)

Like the rest of the newly-built town of Aunay – devastated during the Allied advances in the summer of 1944 – this *Logis* looks handsome in its light-coloured stone livery. Fish dishes feature strongly on the extensive menus: *terrine de poisson, huîtres, filets de St-Pierre à l'oseille* and *coquilles St-Jacques sautées à la Provençale* amongst them.
fpm A–B *meals* C *rooms* 7 A *closed* Mid Sept–mid Oct. Sun evg and Mon (except June–Sept). *post* 14260 Aunay-sur-Odon. Calvados. *phone* (31) 77.63.16.

GOUPILLIERES   Aub. du Pont de Brie
Comfortable rest. with rooms (no showers or baths)/**Secluded**

A small modern building in an isolated site on the west bank of the **Orne**, close to one of the many weirs that are found on the river. It's all simple perfection and it's hardly likely to bankrupt you. The cooking makes great use of the Normandy raw materials – witness some of the specialities: *poulet au cidre, turbot sauce Normandie* and *tarte Normande*.
fpm A–B *meals* C *rooms* 6 A *closed* Mid–end Aug. 1–15 Feb. Wed.
post Goupillières. 14210. Evrecy. Calvados. *phone* (31) 79.37.84.

PONT-D'OUILLY   Commerce
Simple hotel/gardens

For many years this modern *Logis de France* has been well-known for value for money. In the past I've stayed at an annexe called the Clos Fleuri, south of the town on the west bank of the river – I liked it. Regional and classical dishes feature strongly – some examples are: *veau Vallée d'Auge, terrine du chef, tournedos sauce poivre, pintadeau forestière* and *soufflé de brochet*.
fpm A–C *meals* NC *rooms* 15 A–B *closed* 1–15 Oct. Jan. Mon (except mid June–mid Sept). *post* 14690 Pont-d'Ouilly. Calvados. *phone* (31) 69.80.16.

PUTANGES-PONT-ECREPIN   Lion Verd
Simple hotel

A really smart, new stone building, alongside the river and the bridge over the **Orne** – just look for the proud, green lion adorning its walls. The cuisine is totally loyal to Normandy traditions and the raw materials used are fresh as the daisies found in nearby pastures: *andouille de pays, jambon blanc beurre, truite meunière, canard au cidre* and *escalope Vallée d'Auge*.
fpm A–B *meals* C *rooms* 20 A–C *closed* Dec. Jan.
post 61210 Putanges-Pont-Ecrepin. Orne. *phone* (33) 35.01.86.

Digne

VALENSOLE

Moustiers-Ste-Marie

Riez

Verdon

Lac de
Sainte-Croix

Grand Canyon
du Verdon

AUPS

Sillans-la-Cascade

TOURTOUR
Villecroze

Fox-Amphoux

Barjols

SALERNES

Draguignan

COTIGNAC

Argens

Entrecasteaux

Le Thoronet

ROMARIN

The French Riviera is known and loved by millions of people. Yet, I would be prepared to bet a good deal of money to back my claim that perhaps only one car in 5,000 ever ventures north of either the A8 Autoroute or the hectic N7. The Riviera is synonymous with the long strip of Mediterranean coast – visitors to the south tend to want the sea, the sardine-packed sands, the sun and all the other *delights* that go with those holiday pleasures. But to the north of those ribbons of concrete and asphalt is a mass of lovely country, richly rewarding those enterprising enough to seek out its hidden attractions. Invest a small amount of time, even if it is just a day or so, to enjoy those attractions the next time you make the Mediterranean your holiday objective; you'll return often.

I've given the name Var to this chapter; the actual *département* stretches from the mighty River **Verdon** right down to the coast – but I will describe just the northern half of the vast *département*, together with neighbouring parts of the adjoining Alps, both to the north and east of the Verdon.

Let's consider first the scenic pleasures that straddle the river that also shares the name **Var**; you'll see it in the top right-hand corner of the map. The Gorges du Cians is one of the great sights of France – unheard of and unseen by most visitors to the country. A narrow road hugs the walls of the gorge and punches its way through many a rock face as it climbs the steep valley. Towards the northern end, precipitous cliffs overhang the road and come so close together that they nearly touch; dark red rocks add extra splendour to the rushing torrent as it falls steeply down to the River Var.

In the Var Valley is **Entrevaux**, a splendid example of how important a small

132

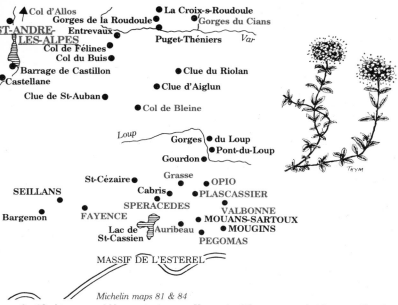

Col d'Allos
Gorges de la Roudoule ●
ST-ANDRE- Entrevaux ●
LES-ALPES
Col de Félines ●
Col du Buis ●
● Barrage de Castillon
Castellane

● La Croix-s-Roudoule
● Gorges du Cians
Puget-Théniers   *Var*

● Clue du Riolan

● Clue d'Aiglun

Clue de St-Auban ●

● Col de Bleine

Loup
Gorges ● du Loup
● Pont-du-Loup
Gourdon ●

Grasse
St-Cézaire ●   ● OPIO
SEILLANS   Cabris ● ● PLASCASSIER
●   SPERACEDES
Bargemon   FAYENCE   VALBONNE
●   ●   ● MOUANS-SARTOUX
Lac de ⛄ Auribeau ● ● MOUGINS
St-Cassien ▽   PEGOMAS

MASSIF DE L'ESTEREL

THYM

Michelin maps 81 & 84

fortified town could be centuries ago. You enter it by a narrow bridge over the river – ramparts surround it and a citadel sits high above the houses.

Puget-Théniers is at the mouth of a *dead-end* valley – don't ignore it; the road up the **Gorges de la Roudoule** terminates in red sandstone cliffs – on your way back down, detour to the *perched* village of **La Croix-s-Roudoule**.

But it is the mass of superb roads to the south of the River Var that I particularly want to bring to your attention. Every single kilometre of those roads has been used, at some time or other, as a stage on the annual Monte-Carlo Rally. You'll be using them in better weather conditions – and, even if it's high summer – you'll have them to yourself. I would suggest you climb south from Entrevaux up the **Col de Félines** and then the fairly recently completed road over the **Col du Buis**. Three dramatic curiosities of Mother Nature should be on your route: the **Clue de St-Auban**; the **Clue du Riolan**; and the **Clue d'Aiglun** (see them in that order).

These *clues* – rifts – have been formed where rivers have literally sliced through the limestone rocks; narrow gorges have a depth of hundreds of metres – all three named above are spectacular sights and should not be bypassed. From the Clue d'Aiglun continue south-west and then climb the magnificent **Col de Bleine**; pine-clad on its northern slopes, it offers such a different Mediterranean perspective on its southern side. If your trip is in May or early June you'll be enchanted by the wild flowers carpeting the green pastures of the valley floors – and yet you are just an hour away from the almost tropical scenery of the coast.

Next, make your way down the infant River **Loup** to the point where it, too, has formed a huge gorge in its fight to reach the sea – the **Gorges du Loup**. You'll see many a tourist on a day trip hereabouts – but don't let that stop you enjoying it all; be sure to explore **Gourdon** – a *perched* village – and be sure to buy some of the splendid jams made at **Pont-du-Loup**.

Grasse is one of my favourite towns in France; its hillside site, high above the coast, makes it a cool, shady haven on unbearably hot days. The narrow streets of the old town, the market, the parks – all combine to give it a fascinating personality. The countryside to the south is an utter delight – fill your eyes with the sheets of colour that cover walls, terraces and gardens: oleander, bougainvilia, veronica and hibiscus. Search out the *perched* villages of **Opio**, **Auribeau**, **Cabris** and **Spéracèdes** – you'll linger long at them all.

As you head generally west, the same prediction can be made when you wander quietly through the streets of three more *perched* villages: **Fayence**, **Seillans** and **Bargemon**. If you want to make detours of a different sort, seek out the caves at **St-Cézaire** and the cool man-made **Lac de St-Cassien**; then climb high up the steep tracks of the red, craggy mountains called the **Massif de l'Esterel** – full of panoramic viewpoints.

Beyond **Draguignan** the hills become more open. With the dramatic exception of one of the great wonders of France – more about that later – the countryside is not as spectacular as the mountains you've left behind you. But there are a series of delights worth seeking out for yourself.

The first of these is the ancient 12th century abbey at **Le Thoronet**; founded by the Cistercians it sits in a secluded, wooded site and amongst its treasures are the church itself, the cloisters and the chapterhouse. A few kilometres to the north, on

Tourtour: the village in the sky!

the other side of the River **Argens**, is the medieval village of **Entrecasteaux** – seen at its best as you approach from the south. Further north still is the village of **Villecroze** – nearby are fine caves, some of which are illuminated. Drive the six kilometres to nearby **Tourtour**, set high amongst the woods to the east. There are several splendid hotels hidden amongst the trees – be sure to enjoy the extensive views their sites and the village provide.

The cascade at **Sillans-la-Cascade** is particularly worth seeing if your visit follows any heavy rain – rare in the summer months. **Cotignac** is a typical village in this part of Var with shady, tree-lined streets, fountains and many a pavement café. But under no circumstances miss the jewel of Fox-Amphoux, 11 kilometres to the north-west. You'll wonder what it costs to retire here and you'll certainly feel pleased with life. One of our visits was in May; my wife and I were captivated by the wild flowers in the fields of these hills – the aroma of herbs and the perfume of those flowers filled our heads!

Barjols should be the last of this series of villages on your route; like Cotignac it has narrow streets, shady squares and dozens of fountains; one of them has an umbrella in the shape of the largest plane tree in Provence. On a hot day you'll certainly tarry long over a cool drink in this charming place.

For our final look at this marvellous, varied expanse of country we must go north to one of the greatest of all the scenic splendours in France – the fantastic Grand Canyon du Verdon. On your way to this majestic sight, drive via **Riez** – the town was important as long as 2,000 years ago; its 7th century baptistry is one of only half a dozen sites still in existence from Merovingian times. Then, passing through fields renowned for the growing of lavender plants, continue to **Moustiers-Ste-Marie**. It has a dramatic site, is famous for its blue pottery, and contains a pottery museum, a chapel and a church amongst its attractions.

Moustiers-Ste-Marie is six kilometres from the mouth of the Verdon Canyon. Below it there's the vast man-made and intense blue **Lac de Sainte-Croix**. To the east lies the 20 kilometres long, deep scar in the limestone plateau; it's a small-scale Grand Canyon of Colorado. Small-scale or not, in Europe it has no rival. In places, the valley floor is over 700 metres below the viewpoints that line the top of the cliffs. The Corniche Sublime runs along the southern line of the canyon's edge; drive it slowly, stop often at the special parking spots, and then walk to the best viewpoints. Don't miss the northern, newer road – the Route des Crêtes.

Follow the Verdon upstream, through old **Castellane**, past the high **Barrage de Castillon**, where another man-made lake provides the river with its first opportunity to produce electricity – and on to **St-André-les-Alpes**. Its name does it justice – its setting is a complete change from those you will have enjoyed earlier. But it's a pity the lake is almost empty these days.

To the north and north-east of St-André-les-Alpes are a series of superb mountain passes. You should try them all, but if time prevents you, let me persuade you to make at least one final drive: continue north, following the infant Verdon to near its source. At that point you'll have no excuse to miss one of the best of all Alpine passes, the mighty Col d'Allos – a dramatic, exhilarating and exciting climb. I promise you will remember the drive for the rest of your life; particularly if you make it in late spring, when the road has just been reopened.

136   The Grand Canyon du Verdon viewed from its northern edge

AUPS   Auberge de la Tour

Comfortable hotel/Quiet

An old, whitewashed building in the northern shadow of the church and hidden
behind two huge trees. Be certain to make the detour to nearby **Tourtour** – the
village in the sky! You'll not miss the **Grand Canyon du Verdon** – but seek out also
tiny **Fox-Amphoux**, to the west. Specialities include *salade verte aux pignons*,
crudités and *gigot de pays grillé aux herbes de Provence*.
fpm A *meals* C *rooms* 24 A–D *closed* Open all the year.
post 83630 Aups. Var. *phone* (94) 70.00.30.

STE-ANDRE-LES-ALPES   Grand Hôtel

Simple hotel/Quiet

Don't be deceived by the name – it's hardly that. It's situated by the small station on
one of the best privately-owned railway lines in France – the metric gauge track
from **Digne** to Nice. The hotel is well placed for you to be thrilled by the mountain
passes to the north – the **Allos** is an exciting climb; you'll relish the scenic solitude
of the high mountain roads.
fpm A *meals* NC *rooms* 24 A–B *closed* Oct–Easter.
post 04170 St-André-les-Alpes. Alpes-de-H.-Prov. *phone* (92) 89.05.06.

SALERNES   Host. Allègre

Simple hotel/Gardens

On the north-west entrance to the village – once called the Grand Hôtel! Amongst
the dishes offered on the menus are *pâté de grives* and *figues au sirop*. An alternative quiet hotel is at **Villecroze** – Le Vieux Moulin (postcode 83690 Salernes); it's
sans restaurant and offers perhaps an even better way of enjoying both the local
countryside and many different restaurants.
fpm A–B *meals* NC *rooms* 25 A–D *closed* 1 Jan–mid Feb. Sun evg and Mon (out of
season). *post* 83690 Salernes. Var. *phone* (94) 70.60.30.

VALENSOLE   Piès

Comfortable hotel/Quiet/Terrace/Gardens

On the **Riez** road and clear of the village. A modern, stone-built hotel high above the
road and with fine views. Classical cuisine. The surrounding countryside is full of
fields with their regimented rows of lavender bushes. Further south it's the turn of
the vine – line after line of them; enjoy the wines that come from them. Valensole is
well-known for its fine almonds.
fpm A–C *meals* NC *rooms* 16 B–C *closed* Thurs (Oct–mid Mar).
post 04210 Valensole. Alpes-de-H.-Prov. *phone* (92) 74.83.13.

VAUCLUSE

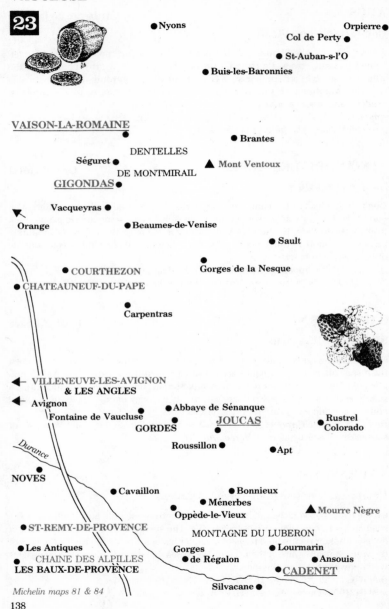

23

● Nyons

Orpierre ●

Col de Perty ●

● St-Auban-s-l'O

● Buis-les-Baronnies

VAISON-LA-ROMAINE
●

● Brantes

DENTELLES

Séguret ● ▲ Mont Ventoux

DE MONTMIRAIL

GIGONDAS ●

Vacqueyras ●

◄ Orange

● Beaumes-de-Venise

● Sault

● COURTHEZON

Gorges de la Nesque

● CHATEAUNEUF-DU-PAPE

●

Carpentras

◄ VILLENEUVE-LES-AVIGNON
& LES ANGLES

◄ Avignon

Fontaine de Vaucluse

● Abbaye de Sénanque

JOUCAS

● Rustrel
Colorado

GORDES

Roussillon ●

● Apt

Durance

NOVES ●

● Cavaillon

● Bonnieux

● Ménerbes

Oppède-le-Vieux

▲ Mourre Nègre

● ST-REMY-DE-PROVENCE

MONTAGNE DU LUBERON

● Les Antiques

● CHAINE DES ALPILLES

LES BAUX-DE-PROVENCE

Gorges

● de Régalon

● Lourmarin

● Ansouis

● CADENET

Silvacane ●

Michelin maps 81 & 84

I never cease to be staggered by the number of people who speed through Provence – their sole objective being to pile up the kilometres as they relentlessly rush to Spain or the Côte d'Azur. Their passion for sticking like leeches to the concrete ribbons called autoroutes forces them to miss some of the greatest pleasures to be found in France. With a minimum amount of effort they, too, could be captivated by this magical countryside – like thousands before them. On balance I'm glad life is like that; it makes it all so much easier for the rest of us to enjoy Provence. But have you got off the beaten track and seen for yourself some of the hidden corners? You will know the famous spots like **Avignon**, **Orange**, Arles and Nîmes; but what of other treasures, both man-made and those sculptured by Nature? My chapter title takes its name from the *département* of Vaucluse – which lies to the east of the River Rhône; the majority of the sights I'll be describing lie within this rich and rewarding *département*.

Elizabeth David gave me the bug for Provence! In her masterpiece *French Provincial Cooking*, she wrote; 'Provence is a country to which I am always returning, next week, next year, any day now.' The dazzling sun, the ochre, gold and terracotta shades of tiles, walls and soil, the pencil-sharp cypresses, the massive, shady plane trees – all combine to lure you, too. You'll savour it for other reasons: it's the market garden of Europe and shopping in its many small village markets is a tonic for any North European or American visitor. A kaleidoscope of colour and texture fills the eyes: aubergines, cauliflowers, asparagus, French beans, olives, onions, garlic, artichokes, tomatoes, courgettes – and many more. The fruit is equally appealing and the Vaucluse takes credit for much of it: melons from **Cavaillon**, mouth-watering table grapes, apricots, peaches, cherries and strawberries; **Apt** has a flourishing glacé fruit industry.

I have divided the chapter into four parts; the first one takes a good look at the countryside lying in the shadow of the mighty **Montagne du Lubéron**. It's a mysterious, sullen mountain – a black mass which shows the other side of the Jekyll and Hyde character of Provence. When the *mistral* blows from the north you'll know only too well why people go mad in these savage hills.

The southern, more sheltered slopes of the Lubéron stretch down to the River **Durance**. To the west of **Cadenet**, on the other bank of that wide, lazy river – it has already earned its keep higher up the valley creating electricity – are the old ruins of a Cistercian abbey at **Silvacane**.

Further west are the **Gorges de Régalon**. You'll have to desert your car to enjoy this natural sight – on really wet days it is not possible to make your way up the narrow, slippery rocks to the cave which is the highlight of your excursion. To the east of Cadenet there's a château at **Ansouis** – it has charming gardens and has been owned by the same family for centuries. There is another château at **Lourmarin**, which is part medieval, part Renaissance.

Looming over all this landscape is the Lubéron. Navigate the narrow lane that runs along its eastern ridge – particularly spectacular are the views from Mourre Nègre, 1125 metres high. To the north of the mountain is a chain of splendid hillside villages: **Bonnieux**, **Ménerbes** and **Oppède-le-Vieux**. Many of the ancient houses have been sympathetically restored by painters, writers and retired folk. I can recall, as I write these words, a picnic my wife and I enjoyed near Bonnieux; the

140   Vaison-la-Romaine: Le Beffroi in the narrow streets of the Haute Ville

produce we had bought earlier, together with a local **Côtes du Lubéron** wine, was perfection in the shady glade we found for ourselves. Apt is an old Roman town – full of interest.

To the north of the Lubéron are several exceptional sights. Close to Apt is the amazing red and ochre village of **Roussillon**. The technicoloured cliffs are dazzling; their stone is quarried to make the walls of the houses in the village. If you want to gasp at the best of the ochre quarries make a *deviation* to the strangely-named **Rustrel Colorado**, north-east of Apt.

Near Roussillon is **Gordes**; the village is best seen from the approach road the D15. Gordes houses the Vasarély Museum but it's in the barren hills to the north and east that you'll find its most intriguing treasures: firstly, the *bories* – small, restored buildings, looking like bee-hives, built in the Stone Age and constructed of dry-stone slabs; and secondly, the old Cistercian **Abbaye de Sénanque** – a sister of Silvacane and Le Thoronet (see *Var*) – where the buildings and a museum explaining the life and topography of the Sahara are particularly interesting.

Finally, west of Gordes is the **Fontaine de Vaucluse** – a thrilling sight in the winter and spring when, after heavy rain, the flow of water is at its strongest: it is a *resurgent spring*; having gone underground kilometres away, it shoots out its flood of water in a spectacular fashion where it exits from the rock face.

My second division takes us further north to the hypnotic sentinel of Provence – the extinct volcano of **Mont Ventoux** (1909 metres). Whenever I am in the area I am drawn inevitably to it. Its lower slopes are covered in pine, beech and oak; higher up, the cool green trees give way to a bare mountain summit – in summer the blistering heat makes it furnace-like. It was here that Tommy Simpson died in 1967 – the most famous of British road cyclists. The narrow roads on the mountain face have seen some epic cycling and motoring hillclimbs during this century. I've driven over it at all times of the year – by day and by night; if you can pluck up courage to do the latter, the fantastic panorama is a spectacle even more amazing than the one you'll gasp at in the daytime.

Every road surrounding or climbing the mountain is exciting motoring; another similar thrilling drive is the **Gorges de la Nesque** road that runs south-west from **Sault**. The roads that encircle and climb over the beautifully-named **Dentelles de Montmirail** to the west of Mont Ventoux are less demanding and show another different face of the Vaucluse. Three villages should lie on your route: **Beaumes-de-Venise**, the home of the honey-tasting, rich Muscat dessert wine; **Vacqueyras** and **Gigondas** come next – both make powerful red wines. This is a corner of Provence where you can feel, taste and smell its unique delights. Finish this small tour of the Dentelles at **Séguret** – a splendid village, full of character and offering fine views of the wine country to the west.

The third part of my chapter considers the attractions of the hills to the north of Mont Ventoux. The gateway to them is **Vaison-la-Romaine**, my favourite small town in Provence – a small-scale Pompeii. Magnificent finds have been made over the years; there are two areas to explore, the Puymin Quarter and the Villasse Quarter. Both contain streets, houses and fountains; there is a Roman theatre and a museum full of precious objects.

To the east of Vaison-la-Romaine are a series of ancient villages, ignored by

141

tourists but, thank heavens, much loved by craftsmen who have brought new life to them: **Brantes**, in the shadow of Mont Ventoux; **Buis-les-Baronnies**, famous for its herb market – no wonder when you breathe in the perfume of the neighbouring hills; **St-Auban-s-l'O** and **Orpierre** – these medieval mountain villages are at either end of the **Col de Perty**. From near the summit of the col you get extensive views. This road from Orange and Vaison across to the Durance is thought to be part of the route that Hannibal used to cross the Alps in 218 BC. It's all marvellous country – quite deserted at any time of the year.

My fourth and last part of this chapter takes you down to the left-hand corner of my map – across the Durance and the Vaucluse *département* border; to the strange outcrop of rocks called the Chaîne des Alpilles. On their northern flanks is another favourite town of mine – **St-Rémy-de-Provence**. Between the hills and St-Rémy are the old Roman ruins called **Les Antiques**. This was once the prosperous town of Glanum. Several interesting parts still remain; amongst them a splendid triumphal arch and a first century mausoleum, built as a memorial to the grandsons of Emperor Augustus. Put aside an hour to explore the excavations at Glanum – they are full of interest; temples, baths and a forum amongst them.

The most famous site in the hills – and sure to be filled with tourists – is **Les Baux-de-Provence**; it's a haunting, ghost-ridden village, *perched* on a hilltop. Over 300 years ago it was a flourishing place; Louis XIII was the individual who ordered the town destroyed. Try to see the craggy hills at dusk; if you are lucky and have the great fortune to revel in the splendour of a Provençal sunset, you'll see the sky looking like a devil's cauldron.

142   Roussillon *perched* on its red and ochre cliffs

CADENET   Aux Ombrelles
Comfortable restaurant with rooms/Gardens

A modern *Logis de France* hiding behind a large willow tree; don't be put off by the
railway line alongside the establishment – it's a single, rusty line and is hardly likely
to worry you. Both food and wine take advantage of the local raw materials: witness
the *asperges du pays, crudités, terrine du chef* and *coq aux Côtes du Lubéron*;
soupe de poisson is an added bonus.
fpm A–D *meals* C *rooms* 11 A–D *closed* Dec. Jan. Mon (out of season).
post 84160 Cadenet. Vaucluse. *phone* (90) 68.02.40.

GIGONDAS   Les Florets
Comfortable hotel/Secluded/Terrace/Gardens

A captivating spot – lost in the hills called **Dentelles de Montmirail**. To the west of
this isolated hotel lies **Gigondas** and a whole mass of wine country. Inevitably the
Gigondas wines feature strongly on the menus – enjoy them with a variety of well-
cooked dishes: *canard à l'orange, lapin au vinaigre* and *pieds paquets maison* are
examples. There's a super terrace for a shady lunch.
fpm A–B *meals* C *rooms* 15 A–D *closed* 1 Jan-mid Feb. Tues evg and Wed (Nov–
Mar). *post* Gigondas. 84190 Beaumes-de-Venise. Vaucluse. *phone* (90) 65.85.01.

JOUCAS   Host. des Commandeurs
Simple hotel

This small *Logis de France* sits at the foot of the village and rewards the visitor with
extensive and commanding views of the vast wall of the **Montagne du Lubéron**, 15
kilometres to the south. Apart from the many scenic splendours that surround the
village you'll also enjoy many good dishes: *jambon cru, cuisses de grenouilles à la
Provençale* and *selle d'agneau grillée* are amongst them.
fpm A–B *meals* NC *rooms* 12 B–C *closed* Jan. Feb. Rest. only: Wed.
post Joucas. 84220 Gordes. Vaucluse. *phone* (90) 72.00.05.

VAISON-LA-ROMAINE   Le Beffroi
Comfortable hotel/Quiet/Terrace/Gardens

An ancient 16th century hotel, lost in the narrow lanes in the Haute Ville; apart from
the many man-made jewels to be found in Vaison itself there are exquisite examples
of Mother Nature's skills to the east. Three interesting and different specialities are
feuilleté de moules au pastis, escalope de haddock à la crème de basilic and
saumon mariné à l'huile d'olive et au romarin.
fpm A–C *meals* C *rooms* 19 A–E *closed* Mid Nov–mid Mar. Rest. only: Mon and Tues
midday (except July–Aug). *post* 84110 Vaison. Vaucluse. *phone* (90) 36.04.71.

VERCORS

24

Veurey-Voroize ●
La Buffe ●
Gouffre Berger ●
La Molière ●
St-Nizier-du-Moucherotte ● ● Grenoble

see page 48

CLAIX ●
CHAMROUSSE →
VARCES ●

Isère

Bourne

●Chorance   ●Villard-de-Lans

Pont-en-Royans ●   ●Gorges de la Bourne
Vernaison
St-Jean-en-Royans ●   ●St-Georges-de-Commiers
Combe Laval ●   Grands Goulets
        ● Les Barraques-en-Vercors

Drac

COL DE LA MACHINE ●   ● La Chapelle-en-Vercors

VERCORS   Corniche
    ST-AGNAN ●   du
Forêt de Lente   Drac
        Gresse-en-Vercors
Col de la Bataille ●   ●Vassieux-en-Vercors   ●

        ●Col de Rousset   ▲ Mont Aiguille

Col de Bacchus ●
    ●Gorges d'Omblèze

        Cirque d'Archiane ●   ● Col de Menée
    DIE ●   *Archiane*

    Saillans
←GRANE   ●   ● Châtillon-en-Diois

    ● Col de la Chaudière   *Drôme*

Le Poët-Laval
●
●DIEULEFIT   *Michelin maps 77 & 81*   **SERRES**
                ↘

144

Together with the *Chartreuse* – to the north-east – this is part of my favourite mountain area of France. The River **Isère** makes two great loops as it tumbles down from the Alps towards the Rhône Valley; on the map it resembles the letter *N*. The right-hand section of the letter *N* contains the Chartreuse; the left-hand area is the **Vercors**. Both areas contain glorious mountain scenery; the craggy peaks are not that high by the standards of the Alps but the hillsides are covered with both ever-greens and deciduous trees and the river valleys – particularly in the Vercors – are full of magnificent sights, fashioned exclusively by Mother Nature. The greatest pleasures of life are free – and this is where you'll find the indisputable proof of that. Use your car to reach the heart of both areas – then desert it and use your feet and lungs.

A few days spent in the two areas – make it a period covering Monday to Friday – is sure to reward you with an inspiring holiday. Both areas are ignored by tourists; it is only at weekends that the folk of **Grenoble** flock into them. I've seen the Vercors at all times of the year. But I enjoy it most in the spring, when the new greens are bursting out and the streams shoot forth their newly-melted water; also in the autumn when the hillsides are a patchwork quilt of colours – differing shades of gold, red, yellow and brown.

My wife and I explored the Vercors, the Chartreuse and the high cols to the south-east of them on one of our very first trips to France; the car we used was our first, an ancient Austin A30 – indeed, it had only cost us £35. It really was in awful condition – the front suspension was literally on its last legs; but it didn't stop us navigating up and down every lane in the Vercors – the more obscure the better. It was not the first time we discovered the terrific pleasure a large-scale map provides; Michelin map number 77 must have cost us pennies in those days but I can't even suggest a figure for the dividends that small, folded piece of printed paper returned. It is just as true today; in completing the research for this book I have revelled in the same mountains, using many of those roads again that we discovered years ago.

That first sortie into the Vercors taught us other valuable lessons – of different kinds. The most humorous lesson – and, this too, is just as true today – was the amazing variety of French plumbing systems you will come across on your travels across the country. We recall a tiny mountain hotel in the Vercors – it's not one of my current recommendations – where the washbasin was of toy-like proportions. The central snorkel-shaped tap that ran ice-cold water (and perhaps once in a while some tepid hot water as well) into the basin was a gigantic size – to make matters worse it had locked solid. Trying to use it as a washbasin was impossible; to com-plicate matters the plumbing was an example of the organ variety – it thumped and thundered. The toilet down the corridor had been built in a space that in all probability had been a cupboard. We both laughed long and hard at the manoeuvres we had to go through with our legs to allow us to use the toilet – *and* close the door!

On another occasion we arrived at a small hotel, when according to Michelin it should have been open. It was shut. Madame was sorry though she was adamant she would prepare something for us. Out of nothing she conjured up a delicious, light meal. A perfect example of how helpful French hotelkeepers can be.

The most serious lesson we discovered all those years ago was the considerable bravery that had been so conspicuously shown by many of the mountain people during the Second World War. I refer to this aspect of recent French history in other

parts of this book but the Vercors is perhaps the most important example. The area is a natural fortress and it truly was a citadel of the Resistance; stop and pay homage at the many roadside monuments where so many were murdered as victims of the Gestapo. It is another area known as *Maquis* country; *Mort pour La France* say the carved words on the simple, small monuments. No finer words can be used for any epitaph. Make certain you seek out the cemetery just north of **Vassieux-en-Vercors**, where hundreds of those brave patriots lie buried.

There are a dozen or more *sites* and *sights* you must on no account miss; I'll deal first with those ones that are situated within the Vercors itself – half a dozen additional ones lie outside its high mountain walls.

Start your exploration by leaving the Isère Valley at **Veurey-Voroize**, just north-west of Grenoble. Climb the narrow, twisting road up to **La Buffe** – it's a pretty run and, just before the Tunnel du Mortier, stop and admire the view that is below you. Continue south to the grassy plateau that goes by the name of **La Molière**; at 1655 metres it provides extensive views to the east. Beneath your feet and to the north, at the **Gouffre Berger**, are some of the most famous and deepest pot-holes in France.

From both **St-Nizier-du-Moucherotte** and near **Villard-de-Lans**, you can make *téléphérique* climbs – the easy way to get to summits around the 2000 metres mark. But it will be your car that will carry you to the best of the Vercors.

West of Villard-de-Lans are three famous natural sights. The most famous of the gorges in the limestone mountains of the Vercors are the ones that have been gouged out by the River **Bourne** – the Gorges de la Bourne. Five kilometres before **Pont-en-Royans** are some fine caves at **Choranche**. South of the Bourne are the

146

amazing Grands Goulets; the tiny, but powerful River **Vernaison** punches itself through the limestone rocks at **Les Barraques-en-Vercors**. Man has built, somehow, an exciting and astonishing road alongside the ferocious stream – a series of tunnels take you through what are known as the Grands Goulets. The third spectacular sight is the Combe Laval – a fantastic *cirque* of rock that rises sharply and steeply above the banks of the Cholet stream. The road that climbs to it from **St-Jean-en-Royans** – a pleasant, sleepy village – is an engineering marvel; ascend it all the way up to the **Col de la Machine**.

From the summit of that col a range of possibilities awaits you. Be sure to spend some hours in the nearby Forêt de Lente. Drive west on secluded roads via the **Col de la Bataille** and the **Col de Bacchus** to the **Gorges d'Omblèze** – another one of my favourite *dead-end* roads in France. Isolated perfection with lovely cascades and forests will be your reward for the effort you make to see them. Just thank heavens that the vast majority of tourists do not bother to make the effort – or haven't a clue that they are there in the first place.

Finish your Vercors trip by leaving it in the south – using the great Col de Rousset. This is one of the great hillclimbs in the Alps – the view from its summit, at the exit of the old tunnel, is one of the most dramatic and extensive in the south of France. Descend to the small town of **Die**.

Die and **Châtillon-en-Diois** are the homes of some of the best *local* wines of France. Die is famous for its sparkling wines; a *demi-sec* **Clairette de Die** (local, *naturel* method) and a *brut* version (very dry and made by the *méthode champenoise*). They are particularly enjoyable when cooled in a mountain stream as an

Looking south from the Col de Rousset: one of the classic French hillclimbs   147

accompaniment to your picnic lunch; you'll find many a suitable spot.

From Die you can probe further south; to the west if the Rhône Valley is your objective, or to the south-east, upstream on the **Drôme**. If Provence is your objective, climb south from **Saillans** up the **Col de la Chaudière** and then descend to a real hidden corner of France; the countryside surrounding **Dieulefit** and **Le Poët-Laval**. At the latter be certain to seek out the ancient *vieux village* – now being so patiently and cleverly restored.

If you leave Die by the other direction, include Châtillon-en-Diois and the nearby **Archiane** Valley in your itinerary; the latter is another *dead-end* road. At the head of the valley is the **Cirque d'Archiane** – another splendid example of an *amphitheatre* of mountains forming a natural barrier.

You may choose to go south now – but I'll make you think long and hard before you do. Why not go north instead from Châtillon-en-Diois. Use the **Col de Menée**; at its summit you'll see, to the north, the astonishing, lurking shape of **Mont Aiguille** – it seems to have a magnetic power over you, as your eyes won't want to leave it. The minor roads to the north of the mountain – around **Gresse-en-Vercors** – are famous for the stages they provide for the Monte-Carlo Rally.

Finally two last pleasures. North-east of Mont Aiguille is the **Drac** Valley – a man-made reservoir. On its eastern side is the **Corniche du Drac** – an enjoyable road that provides you with a fine drive, eventually taking you to **St-Georges-de-Commiers**. At St-Georges is the terminus of a private railway – an exciting *voie métrique* trip up the Drac Valley to La Mure (to the east of the map). Unhappily it only runs on Sundays from June to September.

148

CLAIX   Les Oiseaux
Comfortable hotel/Secluded/Gardens/Swimming pool

A *Relais du Silence* that is well clear of **Grenoble** – the latter is 11 kilometres to the north-east. The hotel is easily reached if you use the new B48 Autoroute that avoids Grenoble. It's a modern hotel, positioned well to enjoy the Vercors and the **Chamrousse** to the east. Cuisine is modest with dishes like *terrine de grives, quenelle de brochet, entrecôte* and *noisette d'agneau* on the menus.

fpm A–B *meals* NC *rooms* 20 B–D *closed* Nov–Jan. Fri and Sat midday (mid Sept–mid Apl). *post* 38640 Claix. Isère. *phone* (76) 98.07.74.

COL DE LA MACHINE   du Col
Simple hotel/Secluded

A simple but modern *Logis de France* at the summit of the road that climbs from **St-Jean-en-Royans** to the top of the magnificent **Combe Laval** – a superb example of a *cirque*. Brave were the men who built this astonishing road and one wonders how they managed to blast those many tunnels near the summit. Enjoy also the **Forêt de Lente** to the south – full of huge evergreens and deciduous trees.

fpm A–B *meals* NC *rooms* 11 A–B *closed* Mid Nov–mid Dec. Mar.
post Col de la Machine. 26190 St-Jean-en-Royans. Drôme. *phone* (75) 45.57.67.

DIE   La Petite Auberge
Comfortable hotel

On the outskirts of Die and with a longstanding reputation for providing good-value meals. Enjoy both the specialities like *pâté chaud* and *truite meunière* and the lovely wines of Die, particularly the sparkling **Clairette de Die** – there are both *demi-sec* and *brut* versions. Head your car up as many of the mountain lanes as you can that climb both north and south from the **Drôme** Valley.

fpm A–C *meals* NC *rooms* 15 B–C *closed* Dec–mid Feb. Sun evg and Mon (except July–Aug). *post* 26150 Die. Drôme. *phone* (75) 22.05.91.

ST-AGNAN   Le Veymont
Simple hotel/Quiet

A lovely spot in the heart of the Vercors. The hotel faces a small church and fountain – all of them set around a tiny village square. Four kilometres to the north is the rebuilt village of **La Chapelle-en-Vercors**, destroyed by the Germans in their battles with the Resistance during the last war. Menus include *truites* (in various forms), *magret de canard* and *tarte tatin*.

fpm A *meals* NC *rooms* 20 B–C *closed* Oct. Nov.
post St-Agnan. 26420 La Chapelle-en-Vercors. Drôme. *phone* (75) 48.20.19.

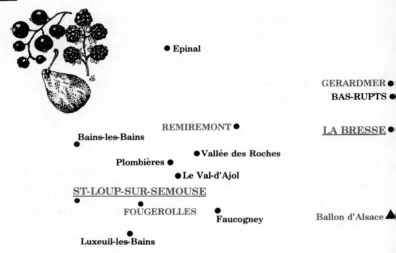

- Epinal

GERARDMER ●
BAS-RUPTS ●

REMIREMONT ●

LA BRESSE ●

Bains-les-Bains
●

● Vallée des Roches

Plombières ●

● Le Val-d'Ajol

ST-LOUP-SUR-SEMOUSE
● ●

FOUGEROLLES ●

● Faucogney

Ballon d'Alsace ▲

●
Luxeuil-les-Bains

▼ Ronchamp

This is an area that is studded with delights of all kinds: wooded hills, tiny lakes, deserted lanes, pleasant small spas in the west and some of the most picturesque wine villages in France on the eastern slopes of the Vosges range. Don't ignore the pleasures of this area; I aim to persuade you to find some time to explore the central and western parts of my map – the eastern string of wine villages are famous enough already.

Vittel and Contrexéville are known by millions as two of the premier spas in France — they lie just to the west of my map: few, however, know the alluring spa towns of **Bains-les-Bains**, **Plombières** and **Luxeuil-les-Bains**.

Saint Colomban established an abbey in Luxeuil in 590 (the Irish monk who founded the abbey at Baume-les-Messieurs – see *Jura*), but long before that, in Roman times, its waters were renowned for their curative benefits. See the Basilique St-Pierre, the ancient house of Cardinal Jouffroy and the Maison François 1er. To the east of Luxeuil is **Faucogney**; to the south and east of here the landscape is peppered with tiny lakes – *étangs* (meres or pools).

An essential diversion from Luxeuil is to world-famous **Ronchamp** – on the N19 and some 20 kilometres north-west of Belfort. Its global fame comes solely from the chapel, the Notre-Dame-du-Haut, designed by Le Corbusier and built in 1955; it sits high above Ronchamp on the northern side of the N19. Long ago it was a place of pilgrimage. In 1913 the first chapel was destroyed by lightning; its neo-Gothic replacement was destroyed in 1944 during the Allied advances. Le Corbusier's chapel, with its concave roof, is an unusual, modern structure; some will hate it, but find the time to enjoy this inspiring, unique spot.

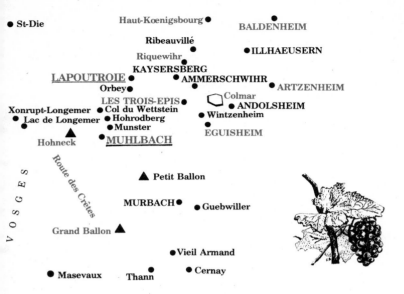

● St-Die   Haut-Koenigsbourg ●   ● BALDENHEIM

Ribeauvillé
Riquewihr ●   ● ILLHAEUSERN
KAYSERSBERG
LAPOUTROIE ●   ● AMMERSCHWIHR
Orbey ●   ● ARTZENHEIM
LES TROIS-EPIS ●   Colmar
Xonrupt-Longemer ● ● Col du Wettstein   ● ANDOLSHEIM
● Lac de Longemer   ● Hohrodberg   ● Wintzenheim
▲   ● Munster
Hohneck   ● MUHLBACH   EGUISHEIM

Route des Crêtes

▲ Petit Ballon

MURBACH ●   ● Guebwiller

Grand Ballon ▲

● Vieil Armand

● Masevaux   Thann ●   ● Cernay

V O S G E S

Michelin map 242

Plombières and Bains-les-Bains are much smaller spas than Luxeuil, but they, too, were established in Roman times. Neither of them are on busy, main roads; both are cool places, surrounded by quiet countryside, ideal for those of you wanting nothing but rest and peace.

You could, and probably would, drive from Plombières to **Remiremont** on the main N57; what a mistake that would be. Instead head south-east to **Le Val-d'Ajol** and then north-east, passing on your route the cascades at Faymont and Géhard and the **Vallée des Roches**. Take care with your navigation – but your efforts will be well rewarded. Remiremont is a biggish place with its splendid Rue Charles-de-Gaulle; arcades line both sides of it.

All the countryside described earlier lies on the gentle western slopes of the Vosges. In early spring its orchards are full of new blossom; the endless splashes of colour will, in time, produce the fruit that is used to such good effect – making the brandies of Alsace called *eaux-de-vie*. These are colourless liqueurs distilled from fermented fruit juices: *poire William* – pear; *mirabelle* – golden plum; *quetsche* – purple plum; *reine-claude* – greengage. Others are distilled from *fraise* – strawberry and *framboise* – raspberry; the most famous being *kirsch* – cherry. **Fougerolles** is the small town most renowned for its production of *alcools blancs* – white alcohols. Fruit liqueurs are not distilled; they are macerated – hence their lovely colours, created by the fruit used to make them.

As we travel east we reach the long north to south range of wooded hills called the **Vosges**. Ignored by so many they hide many delightful scenic spots in the depths of their mysterious, dark pine forests. Take the map-reading care needed to

151

search them out; there are so many of them – I'll highlight some of the more famous ones and some corners that are not so well-known. Let's start in the south and travel north up the ridge of hills, making *deviations* to both east and west, to the lower slopes of the Vosges; but let's leave the wine villages that line the eastern escarpment to the end of this chapter.

The first attraction is the strangely-named **Ballon d'Alsace**. You'll make the trip in your car, but as you wind up the zig-zags think of the torture endured by the cyclists on the Tour de France as they climb those strength-sapping kilometres. At the summit of the Ballon make the short walk to the *table d'orientation* where the panorama, on clear days, can include Mont Blanc.

Descend to **Masevaux** and then head north-east along the Route Joffre, a narrow twisty road that climbs up and descends down several ridges; it's a splendid run – one of the most attractive in the Vosges. At **Thann** there's an exceptional Gothic structure – the Collégiale St-Thiébaut.

At nearby **Cernay** is the start of a spectacular mountain-top run – the **Route des Crêtes**. It climbs steeply up from Cernay; the first essential stop is at **Vieil Armand** – the view is marvellous but also pay your respects at the National Cemetery, situated high above the Alsace Plain. A series of views to both east and west now follows – the most impressive are from the **Grand Ballon**, the highest of the Vosges peaks (1424 metres) and from the **Hohneck** (1362 metres), the latter requiring minimal effort on your part to reach its summit.

In the valleys below this high road – built for strategic purposes during the Great War – lie some of the other varying attractions of Alsace. Both the **Munster** and

South-west of Orbey – typical Vosges countryside

Guebwiller valleys get more and more populated as you continue eastwards down them. Neither of the two towns that give their names to the valleys are too attractive; I much prefer to seek out the quieter, less conspicuous pleasures that straddle the valleys. Take the *dead-end* road to **Murbach** with its lovely 12th century church. The forest roads that encircle the **Petit Ballon** are deserted most of the time; if you want to leave behind all traces of civilisation for an hour or two, these are the lanes you should head your car down.

The same can be said for the marvellous forest roads to the south of **Gérardmer** and **Xonrupt-Longemer** – to the west of the Route des Crêtes. Search out the best example – the one that runs from the **Lac de Longemer** to **Bas-Rupts**. The lakeside town of Gérardmer is a cool, attractive place – its lake offers boating and other water sport pleasures. Just east of the Lac de Longemer is another tiny jewel of a lake, the Lac de Retournemer.

To the north-east of these lakes are three smaller ones – immediately below the eastern boundary of the Route des Crêtes: Lac Vert, Lac Noir and Lac Blanc. From **Orbey**, head south using the pine-scented forest road that runs up to the **Col du Wettstein** and then east to **Les Trois-Epis**. Shortly after leaving the col make the short *deviation* to **Hohrodberg**, a minute place with glorious views to the south. Les Trois-Epis is another cool spot – so quiet and attractive in its lovely forest setting, high above the Alsace Plain, and yet only 14 kilometres from the large town of **Colmar**.

The **Munster** Valley and **Gérardmer** give their names to two of the best Alsace cheeses – the latter is usually called **Gérômé**. Both are soft, gold-coloured cheeses; Munster is stronger than Gérômé and is made in small disks – it's also known for its *knock-out* type of strong smell and apparently it was first made by those 6th and 7th century Irish monks associated with Saint Colomban (he is mentioned once or twice in this book). Many other super local specialities are to be found in Alsace – most having their origins in the days when it was part of Germany. *French Leave* lists most of them – you'll see them on menus everywhere; likewise it also explains all the differing wines of **Alsace** – these take their names from their grape types. All of them are charming, light wines – enjoyable anywhere, but particularly when drunk locally.

You can see the vineyards on the Route du Vin. Before starting this short, enjoyable drive, climb high into the hills north of **Ribeauvillé** to the château at **Haut-Kœnigsbourg**, restored in 1900 by Kaiser Bill the IInd. It's an impressive place with spectacular views to the east. From Ribeauvillé, a series of picturesque wine villages runs in a short chain to the south: **Riquewihr**, **Kaysersberg**, **Ammerschwihr**, **Wintzenheim** and **Eguisheim** are some of them. Medieval Riquewihr is the jewel amongst them; Eguisheim, too, is a delight – walk the narrow streets with flower-laden balconies and windows. Finish your trip by driving into Colmar – parking, thankfully, is easy. The central area of the town is full of treasures: timber houses from the 16th century; the Musée d'Unterlinden – full of medieval exhibits; the Maison Pfister, claimed to be the most beautiful house in the world; an area called Little Venice; and, for the benefit of tourists, pedestrian-only streets in the town centre. Colmar is particularly enjoyable if you explore it in the cool of the evening when you have it to yourself.

154   Eguisheim: one of the villages on the Route des Vins d'Alsace

LA BRESSE
Vallées
Very comfortable hotel/Quiet/Tennis/Lift

A remarkably smart, modern and largish *Logis de France* with every amenity you
could want; considering the prices charged it is exceptional value for money.
Cuisine is of a more modest standard, but so are the prices. Basic stuff like *truites*
(in various ways), *quenelles de homard, poitrine de veau farcie*, the inevitable
choucroute garnie and *vacherin maison*.
fpm A–B *meals* NC *rooms* 65 B–C *closed* Nov–mid Dec.
post 88250 La Bresse. Vosges. *phone* (29) 25.41.39.

LAPOUTROIE
du Faudé
Comfortable hotel/Quiet/Gardens/Swimming pool

An attractive *Logis de France* in the village itself, which thankfully is bypassed by
the main N415 to the east. Bedrooms are in a modern annexe behind the restaurant.
The hotel is well placed for you to enjoy the hills and lakes to the south-west and all
the nearby wine villages to the east. *Choucroute royale, foie gras* and *coq au
Riesling* are amongst the local dishes on offer.
fpm A–D *meals* NC *rooms* 25 A–C *closed* Jan. Wed evg and Thurs.
post 68650 Lapoutroie. H.-Rhin. *phone* (89) 47.50.35.

MUHLBACH
Perle des Vosges
Comfortable hotel/Quiet/Gardens

A largish *Logis de France* in a super site, high above the village of Muhlbach with
extensive and fine views southwards to the two **Ballon** peaks. Muhlbach is in the
Munster Valley, famous for its soft, gold-coloured, strong-tasting cheese. Menus
allow you to try many alternatives: *bisque d'écrevisses, escalope de veau aux
chanterelles, médaillon de chevreuil aux airelles*.
fpm A–C *meals* NC *rooms* 25 A–D *closed* Nov–mid Dec.
post Muhlbach. 68380 Metzeral. H.-Rhin. *phone* (89) 77.61.34.

ST-LOUP-SUR-SEMOUSE
Trianon
Simple hotel/Terrace

An old building (and the fourth *Logis de France* recommended by me in the Vosges)
which overlooks the River Semouse and is away from the busy part of the small
town. No great effort made to offer regional dishes; but you'll find *confit de canard,
pintadeau aux girolles, truite Val de Semouse* and *grenouilles sautées*. Explore the
many small spa towns to the north.
fpm A–C *meals* NC *rooms* 10 B–C *closed* Feb. Rest. only: Sat (Oct–Mar).
post 70800 St-Loup-sur-Semouse. H.-Saône. *phone* (84) 49.00.45.

INDEX OF PLACES – referred to in the area texts and shown on area maps